Men-at-Arms • 42

The King's German Legion

Otto Von Pivka • Illustrated by Michael Roffe

Series editor Martin Windrow

First published in Great Britain in 1974 by Osprey Publishing,
Midland House, West Way, Botley, Oxford OX2 0PH, UK
44-02 23rd St, Suite 219, Long Island City, NY 11101, USA
Email: info@ospreypublishing.com

Osprey Publishing is part of the Osprey Group.

Transferred to digital print on demand 2010

First published 1974
3rd impression 2005

Printed and bound by PrintOnDemand-Worldwide.com, Peterborough, UK

A CIP catalogue record for this book is available from the British Library

ISBN: 978 0 85045 192 4

Series Editor: Martin Windrow

The Woodland Trust
Osprey Publishing is supporting the Woodland Trust, the UK's leading woodland conservation
charity, by funding the dedication of trees.

www.ospreypublishing.com

The Origins of the Legion

Like Sir Tristram of King Arthur's legendary court, the King's German Legion was born in sorrow, their particular tragedy being the occupation of their homeland, the Electorate of Hanover, by a 13,000-strong French force under General Mortier in 1803. Ever since the line of the House of Welfen (the traditional rulers of Hanover) had been transplanted into the British Isles in the person of George I in 1714, a personal union had existed between Britain and Hanover (of which the British kings were Electors).

Hostilities between Britain and various continental powers (mainly France) had led to various difficulties for Hanover. In 1801 the Electorate had been occupied by Prussia, and ever since large revolutionary French armies had been lurking near her borders. It was obviously only a question of time before the blow fell, and the morale of the Hanoverians was low because they knew that they could expect no help from England since she was preoccupied with thwarting Napoleon's threatened mastery of the European continent.

As a result of the apparent hopelessness of their political situation, the Hanoverians had neglected their army and their fortresses. Many of the regiments existed only on paper and the state of training and readiness of the few available men left much to be desired. The Electorate's main fortress, Hamelin, was old and had been neglected for years and the government of Hanover had adopted the ostrich technique of ignoring the threatening developments on their borders in the hope that they would vanish like a bad dream.

In May 1803 the Hanoverian army consisted of 15,546 men – cavalry, infantry, artillery and engineers – but of these, more than one-third were *Beurlaubten* (on more or less permanent leave). On the 11th of that same month, Talleyrand (the French Foreign Minister) had informed the British Ambassador that unless British rearmament ceased forthwith, the First Consul would be forced to send 20,000 men to Holland and, as Hanover was near by, it was 'natural' that they would take up a camp on the Electorate's borders.

The Prime Minister of Hanover, von Lenthe, refused to take any action upon receiving news of this clear threat to the integrity of his state. An easy French victory was thus prepared.

At the last moment the Hanoverian forces were mobilized under command of Field-Marshal Wallmoden, but von Lenthe's government acted almost as if they were in the pay of the French and hindered almost every move.

Major von der Decken of the Hanoverian Army was sent secretly to Berlin to enlist Prussian aid for the Anglo-Hanoverian cause, but without success. Russia then informed Prussia that if Prussian troops occupied Hanover again, Russia would take this as an act of war against herself and would react accordingly.

The Duke of Brunswick, Commander-in-Chief of the armies of the Holy Roman Empire (or German Confederation), refused a Hanoverian request for aid in the case of a French attack, and Hanover was thus left very much on her own.

For an unexplained reason, the Hanoverian intelligence of the opposing French Army was very bad: the potential invaders consisted of not more than 13,000 men, badly equipped and completely without artillery and with only a few poorly mounted squadrons of cavalry; the Hanoverian rumour increased this force to 30,000 men.

On 1 June 1803 the Duke of Cambridge assumed command of the 4,000-strong Hanoverian forces assembled at Nienburg. Total mobilized Hanoverian forces were 2,700 cavalry and 6,300 infantry. The French, under General Mortier, invaded Hanover and were met by a deputation

British infantry drilling early in the first decade of the nineteenth century. They appear to wear some kind of light-coloured drill jacket rather than the scarlet coatee of normal service dress. In 1804–5 the infantry and foot artillery of the King's German Legion were based at Hilsea Barracks, Portsmouth, while the cavalry and horse artillery were trained at a separate depot at Weymouth

sent by the Hanoverian Government who agreed that the Hanoverian Army would not take up arms against the French in the forthcoming war. The Duke of Cambridge, learning of this, left at once for England in disgust.

The dithering and dallying of the Hanoverian Government continued as did Mortier's advance, and on 2 June 1803 there was the first clash of the campaign at the village of Borstel where the French, after having taken prisoner a Hanoverian officer and trumpeter (who had advanced under a flag of truce), were checked by Hanoverian cavalry. The 9th and 10th Hanoverian Dragoons, a company of light infantry and two guns threw the French back. This was to be the only clash of the 1803 campaign.

General von Hammerstein, commanding the Hanoverian advanced guard, now withdrew over the River Weser because he felt himself too weak to remain west of that obstacle in the face of the larger French force.

On 3 June the Convention of Suhlingen was signed between the Hanoverian deputies (von Bremer, a court official, and Oberstleutnant von Bock, commander of the Leibgarde-Regiment) and Mortier.

This Convention demanded that the Hanoverian Army should withdraw east over the River Elbe and deliver up its artillery to the French. This was done.

On 15 June news was received that Napoleon had refused to accept the Suhlingen Convention and that hostilities were to recommence. Thus, by a series of tricks and bluffs, the French were now in possession of almost all of Hanover at the cost of one minor cavalry skirmish.

Plans were prepared in England to send ships to the Elbe to bring out the Hanoverian Army but events overtook these plans.

A second convention was now prepared by General Alexander Berthier, Napoleon's Chief of Staff. It was short:

1. The Hanoverian troops will withdraw over the Elbe, lay down their weapons and be taken to France. They will retain all their baggage, the officers their swords and the latter may choose a place of residence on the continent but may not go to England.

2. The Hanoverian Army may march past with all the honours of war. Arrangements will be made for the feeding of the men and the transport of the baggage.

3. This capitulation shall be valid without requiring the ratification of either government.

Von Lenthe had already warned Wallmoden to accept these terms. At this point Wallmoden commanded 2,000 cavalry, 7,000 infantry and fifty three-pounder 'Amusettes' or light regimental artillery and some howitzers. They were cut off

4

from all sources of reinforcement or supply and the howitzers had been permitted him by the French general as *pièces d'honneur*. His ammunition would last for two days' action at normal rates. Mortier had 13,000 men, but his logistical situation was vastly better than his opponent's.

Wallmoden called a council of war and it was decided to fight, but before action occurred von Lenthe arrived at his headquarters bearing a new, revised capitulation which held better terms. The fight was delayed, morale slumped, the men became uneasy and the moment for action slipped away.

It was finally arranged that Wallmoden and Mortier should meet in a boat anchored in the middle of the River Elbe to sign the revised convention, and this was done on 5 July 1803 near the village of Artlenburg. Under the terms of this treaty the Hanoverian Army was disbanded.

King George III refused to ratify the Elbe Convention, and thus the former members of his army were not bound by the third clause which stated that they would not serve against France until they had been exchanged for a similar number of captured Frenchmen.

By 28 July 1803 von der Decken (who had now been promoted to lieutenant-colonel) was in England and had secured letters patent from the King to raise a 'King's German Regiment' formed of foreigners including ex-members of the Hanoverian Army. Its strength was not to exceed 4,000 men.

Due to von der Decken's personal unpopularity in Hanoverian circles and to the fact that many potential recruits were deterred from joining because they feared that, once in English uniform, they would be shipped off to one of the far-flung colonies to die of yellow fever or some other plague, recruits were initially slow in coming forward.

There was a conditional clause in von der Decken's patent: if the corps had not reached a strength of 400 within three months it would be disbanded.

The recruits came in a thin trickle until the end of September 1803 and even this trickle was admirable considering the obstacles and perils which recruiters and recruits had to overcome in Hanover.

The first depot of the regiment in England was at Lymington near Portsmouth, but this was soon too small and they were moved to the Isle of Wight. Command was first vested in Major von Hinüber who had already distinguished himself in British service in India. He took over on 13 October 1803 on the Isle of Wight.

The French meanwhile had not been idle in occupied Hanover. As well as hindering the recruitment for the 'King's German Regiment', they were actively canvassing for their own 'Légion Hannovrienne'.

A measure of their success can be gained from the fact that only three former officers of the Hanoverian Army joined this Legion (a lieutenant and two ensigns), and one of these was a Danish subject by birth! The Légion Hannovrienne consisted of infantry (clothed in red with dark blue facings) and cavalry (dark green with yellow facings). Apart from Hanoverians, its 1,400 men included a large majority from many other nations; it was disbanded in 1811, its members going into the 127th French Line Infantry Regiment which was recruited of Germans in and around Hamburg.

The Organization of the Legion

On the same day that von der Decken received his patent to raise the King's German Regiment, a Scottish officer (recently out of Dutch service), Major Colin Halkett, was given permission to raise a similar foreign corps for English service. It was to be a battalion of 459 men initially, but if he succeeded in increasing it to 800 men he was to be promoted lieutenant-colonel.

On 3 October 1803 the King's German Regiment had 450 men and its future was thus secure. In fact, things looked so promising that the original patent was extended to embrace a corps of all arms (cavalry, artillery, engineers and infantry) whose strength was not to exceed 5,000 men.

Former members of the Hanoverian Army were now streaming into England via Heligoland and thus the training of specialists, such as artillerymen, was no problem.

In mid-November 1803 the King's German Regiment was moved from the Isle of Wight to Hilsea Barracks, Portsmouth (a camp which in 1952 still held British soldiers). Their strength now was about 1,000 men and they were organized into two light infantry battalions and a battalion of line infantry. Cadres for the horse artillery and cavalry were training separately in Weymouth, the foot artillery were in Hilsea Barracks. By the end of 1803 one horse and one foot battery had been formed. The cavalry were organized into four squadrons of heavy and four of light dragoons and by February 1804 each arm was increased to six squadrons of 450 sabres. Living in Weymouth and Dorchester and commanded by Major-General von Linsingen, they were popular with the King, who often appeared in the uniform of the heavy dragoons.

On 19 December 1803 the King's German Regiment had been combined with Halkett's foreign corps and was henceforth known as the 'King's German Legion'. The overall command of the Legion was given to Adolph, Duke of Cambridge, who was very popular with the Hanoverians due to his previous connection with them.

During its existence over 15,000 men entered

Cap-plate of the line battalions of the Legion, 1812–16. Although no example of the plate worn on the earlier ('stovepipe') shako is known to survive, it was probably identical, or very similar, to this. The battalion number is embossed in the centre of the oval belt bearing the Legion's title. (Actual example in Bomann Museum, Celle, Germany)

the King's German Legion and of these 75·5 per cent were Hanoverians (42 per cent were members of the old Electoral Army), 17 per cent were Germans of other states and only 7·5 per cent were 'foreigners'.

The artillery and cavalry in particular were almost purely Hanoverian while the two light battalions contained the highest percentage of 'foreigners'.

In April 1804 the 2nd Line Infantry Battalion of the Legion was raised and in May the 3rd. The 2nd Foot Artillery Battery was completed in July and the formation of a second horse artillery and third foot artillery battery was begun.

By January 1805 the King's German Legion consisted of the following units:

Cavalry Brigade
Major-General von Linsingen
1st Regiment of Heavy Dragoons –
Colonel von Bock
1st Regiment of Light Dragoons (Hussars) –
Colonel Viktor von Alten

Light Infantry Brigade
Colonel von Alten
1st Light Battalion – commanded by the brigadier
2nd Light Battalion – Lieutenant-Colonel Halkett

First Line Brigade
Colonel von Barsse
1st Line Battalion – Colonel von Ompteda
2nd Line Battalion – commanded by the brigadier

Second Line Brigade
Colonel von Langwerth
3rd Line Battalion – Colonel von Hinüber
4th Line Battalion – commanded by the brigadier

Artillery
Commander – Colonel von der Decken (also Adjutant-General of the Legion)
Major Friedrich von Linsingen
1st Horse Artillery Battery –
Captain G. J. Hartmann
2nd Horse Artillery Battery – Captain Röttiger
1st Foot Artillery Battery – Captain Brückman
2nd Foot Artillery Battery – Captain Kuhlmann
3rd Foot Artillery Battery – Captain Heise

Engineers
Captains Berensbach, Prott and Meinecke
Lieutenants Hassebroik, Appuhn and Schweitzer

For internal use, drill commands were given in German, English being used only on large parades and manœuvres.

In July 1805 at Weymouth the Cavalry Brigade and Captain Hartmann's horse artillery battery were part of an 8,000-strong corps in an exercise camp under command of the Duke of Cumberland. The Germans were by no means behind their English comrades when it came to demonstrating martial skills.

In February 1806, in north Hanover, the 2nd Heavy Dragoons and the 3rd Light Dragoons were raised: each was about 500 men strong, and the 2nd Light Dragoons was brought up to the same strength.

Each existing infantry battalion was increased to 1,000 men strong and 5th, 6th and 7th Line Battalions were formed.

Three hundred men were engaged to form the cadre of the 8th Line Battalion and a 4th Foot Battery was raised for the artillery. In mid-February 1806 the expeditionary force was re-embarked from Hanover and returned to Portsmouth where the cavalry, the three newly raised infantry battalions and the artillery disembarked. The two light battalions and the 1st, 2nd, 3rd and 4th Line Battalions sailed on to Ireland. They were followed in April by the 1st Heavy and the 1st Light Dragoons, who embarked in Liverpool for Dublin.

The 2nd Heavy Dragoons went to Northampton under Colonel von Veltheim; the 2nd Light Dragoons were in Canterbury under Colonel Viktor von Alten. The 3rd Light Dragoons, under Colonel von Reden, were in Guildford. All the cavalry of the Legion were mounted on English horses even though many Hanoverian horses had been bought in the Electorate during the expedition. The 5th and 6th Infantry Battalions formed the 3rd Line Brigade under Colonel Dreiberg and were posted to Winchester where they were joined in May by the 4th Line Brigade (7th and 8th Line Battalions) under Major-General von Drechsel. The artillery was in Porchester commanded by Major Röttiger.

A word here as to the status of the Legion in relation to the British Army: although the officers of the Legion received their commissions from George III, they were not part of the British Army and were considered inferior to British officers in that they belonged to a 'foreign corps'.

The 1st Line Brigade was soon moved from Ireland to Gibraltar, which place they reached at the end of June 1806. The 3rd Line Brigade took their place in Ireland.

The Legion enjoyed its stay in the Emerald Isle even though their visit was marred by the clash at Tullamore (in July 1806) when fighting, of a serious nature, broke out between Irish militia units and the Legion. A subsequent court of inquiry found the Germans to be absolutely blameless in this affair.

The
Battle History of the Legion

In November 1805 came news that the Legion was to contribute men to form part of an expedition to land in Hanover as part of the Anglo-Austro-Russian war effort against Napoleon, who had pulled most of his troops southwards out of northern Germany. Six thousand men of the Legion sailed with Lord Cathcart's force of 18,000 in November 1805. They were investing Hamelin, the only French strongpoint in the Electorate, when the news of Napoleon's triumph at Austerlitz (2 December 1805) was followed by the order to withdraw.

A confused political situation in Europe, and the death of William Pitt, were exploited by Napoleon with his usual inventiveness. Prussia eventually declared war on France, and the British Foreign Minister Canning sent a force to Swedish Pomerania in June 1807. It included the 1st Division of the Legion (Major-General von Drechsel) and the 2nd Division (Major-General von Linsingen), which landed on the island of Rügen in early July – only to have their hopes dashed by the Peace of Tilsit between France and Russia (7–9 July 1807). The units involved were the 1st and 2nd Light and 3rd–8th Line Battalions, the 2nd and 3rd Light Dragoons, and four artillery batteries. These units were pulled out and sent to join another expeditionary force, this time to Denmark. Signs that this powerful maritime nation might become an active ally of France prompted a British pre-emptive operation. Lord Cathcart's total force of about 26,000 included some 10,000 of the Legion; the 1st and 2nd Line Battalions and the 2nd Hussars, from Gibraltar and Ireland respectively, joined the elements from Rügen. The Legion infantry formed the 2nd Division under the Earl of Rosslyn.

Copenhagen had a garrison of some 14,000, and about 11,000 other Danish troops were in the area. These were driven off, and the first assault went in on 24 August 1807, with the Legion well to the fore. Bombardment of the city began on 2 September, and Copenhagen capitulated five days later. The Danish fleet, and a total of about five million pounds sterling in assorted booty, fell into British hands. Prize-money was paid to the men of the expeditionary force, according to rank: privates received £2, lieutenants £47 and generals £1,500. The fleet was loaded, and weighed anchor on 21 September. Several ships were lost in a storm during the return voyage, and with them some 700 officers and men of the 1st, 2nd and 7th Line Battalions of the Legion, drowned or stranded and captured. Total Legion losses in the Danish expedition were thirty-six officers and 1,139 men – a tenth of the total strength – but 1,438 new recruits had been obtained in Hanover.

While the remainder of the Legion stayed in England after this campaign, the 3rd, 4th, 6th and 8th Line Battalions were among units who took ship for Lisbon. Half the expedition's ships were forced to put about by a Biscay storm; the remaining troops found the French in Lisbon before them, and eventually reached Sicily, via Gibraltar, on 24 March 1808. They had been at sea for five months. In April another expedition to the Baltic was mounted, and the Legion contributed the 3rd Hussars, the light battalions and the 1st, 2nd, 5th and 7th Line Battalions. Sir John Moore's force rode at anchor in Gothenburg harbour for six weeks and then returned to England; he had been unable to agree on any operational plans with the Swedish King. On 31 July 1808 this force was ordered to sail for Portugal to reinforce the army which Sir Arthur Wellesley was leading to liberate that country, occupied by the French but now seething with rebellion at the news of the great risings against Napoleon and his puppet-king brother, Joseph, in Spain. Moore's force eventually landed at the mouth of the Maceira River on 25 August.

Wellesley had already won the Battle of Vimiero (21 August 1808), and the French commander, Junot, was suing for peace. Junot succeeded in persuading Wellesley's new superior, Sir Hugh Dalrymple, to conclude the infamous Convention of Cintra, whereby 24,000 French troops were shipped home from Portuguese harbours – in *British ships* – with all their weapons, baggage and booty. The storm of acrimony which burst in England at the news cost Dalrymple his career and Wellesley a period in the political and military wilderness; Moore took over command in Portugal. He received orders to take 35,000 men into Spain to relieve French pressure on the makeshift Spanish armies, which were suffering a series of staggering blows as Napoleon reinvaded their country.

Moore found no Spanish forces in being with which he could co-operate. Madrid fell to Napoleon on 4 December 1808, and the French

Belt-plate of the line battalions, 1803–16. Again, an actual example in the Bomann Museum; it is rather surprising that the plate carries no indication of any particular battalion

turned on Moore's army, now dangerously isolated. Among his regiments were the 3rd Hussars of the Legion, representing a third of his entire cavalry, and the 1st and 2nd Light Battalions. The army made a grim forced march north-west through the Galician mountains to the ports of Corunna and Vigo, hotly pursued by greatly superior French forces. The 3rd Hussars distinguished themselves at Benavente on 29 December, in the course of one of the few rearguard actions which Moore permitted his harassed army to fight. They threw back an attack across the Esla River by the Chasseurs à Cheval of the Imperial Guard, and the French commander, General Lefebvre-Desnouettes, was captured by Trooper Bergmann of the Legion.

The two light battalions and the 2nd Hussars of the Legion took part, in the second half of 1809, in the ill-fated Walcheren expedition. This futile exploit, which cost the lives of an average of thirty-five men a day from disease alone, was finally brought to a merciful close in December 1809.

The 3rd, 4th, 6th and 8th Line Battalions and the 3rd Foot Battery had landed in Sicily in April 1808 with Major-General Spencer's force of 7,000. They took part in several actions aimed at harassing the French puppet Kingdom of Naples, including a very successful raid on the mainland in the summer of 1809, and an equally impressive defence of the island against an invasion by Murat in September 1810. But the main theatre of the Mediterranean war, and one in which the Legion was to earn undying renown, was the Peninsula.

With Wellington in the Peninsula

In April 1809 Wellesley re-entered Portugal just as the French were about to invade that country with three armies. In the north was the first army under Marshal Soult, a second under Victor was on the River Tagus and Ney stood in Galicia with the Third or Reserve Army. In eastern Spain was a further army under Marshal St Cyr; only the southern provinces were still under control of the rebels.

Soult invaded Portugal, occupied Oporto and then remained static for a month during which Wellesley collected together an Anglo-Portuguese army of over 25,000 men including 3,300 men of the King's German Legion; sixty men of the 3rd Hussars (Captain Meyer); the 2nd and 4th Foot Batteries (Captains Rettberg and Heise); the 1st Line Brigade (under Major-General Langwerth) consisting of the 1st and 2nd Line Battalions (Major Bodecker and Lieutenant-Colonel Brauns); and the 2nd Line Brigade (under Colonel von Löw) consisting of the 5th and 7th Line Battalions.

On 7 May, Wellesley moved north: the French concentrated under Soult in Oporto, and destroyed the pontoon bridge over the Douro leading to the English-held south bank. All local boats were also brought to the north side of the river – all except one which the British found and used to ferry men across the Douro, one mile upstream of Oporto.

By the time the French discovered what was going on, a flotilla of boats was being used to build up the British bridgehead, and this force repelled Soult's attacks. Soult then withdrew over the mountains into Spain, losing all his artillery and baggage-train en route. The French losses were 6,000 men and fifty-eight guns. North Portugal had thus been cleared of its oppressors and Sir John Moore's defeat amply revenged.

News now reached Wellesley that Lisbon was threatened by the corps of Victor and Lapisse and he at once had to move his army south again. On 27 June they reached Abrantes on the south bank of the River Tagus and were joined by 5,000 reinforcements from England which included 600 men of the 1st Hussars of the Legion, who were brigaded with the 23rd Light Dragoons under General Anson.

By 10 July Wellington had moved his army over the Spanish border to the fortress of Plasencia in order to co-operate with General Cuesta's Spanish Army. The Spaniards had 32,000 men, but their quality lagged far behind their numerical strength.

Wellesley's attempts to co-operate with Cuesta were doomed to failure due to the senility and pride of that general; an Allied attack was arranged against the French at Talavera de la Reyna on 23 July and the British troops had been under arms, waiting to advance for three hours before a message arrived from Cuesta to say that he would not fight that day as it was Sunday! Next day the Spaniards mounted an independent attack against Victor and were bloodily repulsed. Cuesta finally realized that his powers were limited and placed himself under Wellesley's command; the combined armies now advanced against the French and on 27 July the Battle of Talavera was begun.

Wellesley's Anglo-German-Portuguese force was 20,000 men and thirty guns strong, the Spaniards had 32,000 men and seventy guns. On the French side were the following corps: Sebastiani (17,500 men), Victor (23,000) and the troops of King Joseph's guard from Madrid (5,800 men). The French artillery had eighty guns. Many of the men in the French corps were Germans from Napoleon's 'Confederation of the Rhine' (e.g. Leval's division).

The battle lasted two days and ended with the withdrawal of the French. Although left in control of the battlefield, Wellesley's position was critical because of the total failure of the Spanish Junta to provide the logistic support which they had promised, and the approach of fresh French armies. He had to withdraw into Portugal again.

Losses in this battle were severe on both sides; the Anglo-German-Portuguese had 5,363 casualties, and of these 1,407 belonged to the King's German Legion. This represented 42 per cent of the Legion's strength on the days of the battle. The English troops lost 23 per cent of their battle strength.

The French losses were 10,000 men, of which 1,000 came from the Germans of the Confederation of the Rhine Division whose total battle strength was only 3,100 men.

The effects of the Battle of Talavera for the Legion were most positive: they were now accepted as comrades by the British soldier, and by the British public as part of the British Army.

A London Opposition newspaper which published an article unjustly defaming the Legion was arraigned by the Government and the publisher sent to prison for two years and fined £1,000.

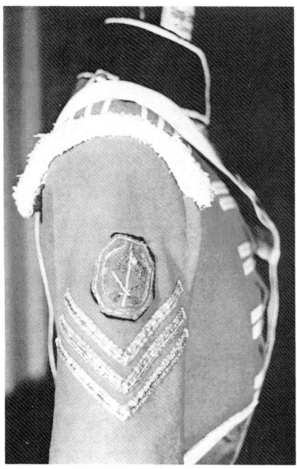

Detail of the uniform of a colour-sergeant of the Light Company, 7th Line Battalion, preserved in the Bomann Museum. The white worsted fringe of the dark blue shoulder-strap can just be seen under the sword-belt: the strap is edged with half-inch white tape. The chevrons are silver, the octagonal badge patch is edged in dark blue, and the ground of the patch is uniform red. It is no longer possible to tell if the woven detail was gold or silver. The flag shown is a battalion colour, dark blue with the Union flag in the top corner. Note that the field of the 'wing' is red, not dark blue as shown by Beamish and Schwertfeger and subsequently copied by Knötel

Withdrawal: Autumn 1809

On 2 August Wellesley found that Soult was at Plasencia with 40,000 men, threatening to cut him off from Portugal. Immediate withdrawal was essential, and a most punishing series of forced marches – during which ammunition and baggage had to be abandoned to make wagon-space for sick and wounded – brought the hungry and exhausted army to Merida on 24 August. After a few days' rest the march was resumed, and the Spanish citadel of Badajoz was reached on 4 September. This area was damp and unhealthy, and Wellington (he had been raised to the peerage for his victory at Talavera) soon moved his army north into the healthier, and friendlier Portuguese countryside along the Mondego River. Meanwhile the Spanish armies continued to suffer regular defeats through insisting on facing Napoleon's veteran soldiers and experienced generals in head-on battles.

While his army was rested, drilled and reinforced in readiness for the inevitable French attempt to reinvade Portgual in the next campaigning season, Wellington began the construction of the great triple line of defences known as the Lines of Torres Vedras. This system of mutually supporting forts and redoubts turned the Lisbon peninsula into one great citadel into which civilians and livestock could be brought in the face of invasion. The French, largely dependent on living off the land, were to be presented with a deep belt of 'scorched earth'. Meanwhile the Light Division watched the French and guarded the fords of the Agueda River; for this demanding scouting duty General Craufurd received the 1st Hussars of the Legion, widely considered to be the most professional and reliable cavalry unit in the entire army. This link between the Hussars and the 'Light Bobs' was to continue.

The 1810 Campaigns

When the French finally moved, Ney attacked the northern 'corridor' into Portugal and invested the key fortress of Ciudad Rodrigo while Mortier threatened Badajoz and the southern route. Hill's corps was sent towards Badajoz while Wellington took the main army – including the Legion units – north. Ciudad Rodrigo could not be relieved without unduly endangering the field army, and fell on 10 July 1810. Wellington's plans were rather upset by the unexpectedly quick fall of the Portuguese fortress of Almeida, but he conducted a masterly retreat in the face of the French Army of Portugal. Now commanded by Napoleon's luckiest and boldest marshal, Masséna, this consisted of three corps: between them Ney, Junot and Reynier had 66,000 infantry and 8,000 cavalry. Wellington had 48,000 infantry and 3,000 cavalry, and half his army was made up of the untried Portuguese regiments which General

Beresford had been reorganizing for more than a year. Their quality was soon to be confirmed.

While the Portuguese civilians fell back into the Lines of Torres Vedras behind him, burning what they could not carry, Wellington withdrew under perfect control, and reached Busaco ridge on 25 September. This was an area he had picked out, and improved by judicious road-building, months beforehand. Two days later the Battle of Busaco was fought between the Allied army of 24,000 British and 25,000 Portuguese, and the corps of Junot and Reynier. By maximum use of the ground, and superior British firepower, the Allies easily defeated repeated French assaults on the ridge. The Portuguese withstood their baptism of fire excellently; French losses were between 5,000 and 6,000 men, while the Allies lost only 1,000. Legion losses were three officers and forty-seven men dead and wounded.

Masséna eventually outflanked the Busaco position, and the Allies continued to fall back on the Lines of Torres Vedras. By mid-October they were safely inside, and reinforced by fresh British drafts and two of the more reliable Spanish divisions under General La Romana. Masséna was taken by surprise, and quickly realized that he was not going to achieve his expected victory by a frontal assault on the massive fortifications. His army sat down in the desert so carefully prepared for them, and proceeded to starve to death. His pleas for support eventually brought 12,000 reinforcements, who merely ate up the available provisions more quickly. In March 1811 he began his inevitable retreat, and Wellington, strengthened by 7,000 fresh troops from England and a supply fleet, prepared to follow on his heels.

1811: Barossa and Albuera

The Spanish Junta in southern Spain had been forced to move from Seville to Cadiz and set up their capital there. Soult sent Victor and his corps to besiege the port, and the Spanish garrison of 21,000 was reinforced by General Graham and 8,000 British troops, including two squadrons of the 2nd Hussars of the Legion. When Soult had to send strong drafts to support Masséna, in

January 1811, the garrison took the opportunity to launch a raid on the besiegers. The Hussars were among 4,500 British troops under Graham and 10,000 Spaniards under La Peña who left Cadiz by sea and landed at Tarifa, behind enemy lines, on 1 March 1811. Prospects were encouraging, but unfortunately La Peña was in overall command, and even though Victor could only field 7,000 men, the sight of so many Frenchmen paralysed the Spanish general.

On 5 March the Allied army had reached the heights of Barossa and Graham's men immediately engaged the 7,000 French who were opposed to them. In spite of repeated requests for help, La Peña remained inactive to the rear of the struggle with the great part of his Spanish force.

At one critical moment, after the British infantry were in a disorganized state having just thrown back a French assault, French cavalry was about to charge them in the flank when the 2nd Hussars of the Legion rushed on to the enemy cavalry, broke them and captured two cannon. This sealed the British victory; in the two-and-a-half-hour battle the French had lost over 2,400 men; Generals Ruffin and Rousseau, eighteen officers and 420 men had been captured as had been one eagle (that of the 8e Ligne) and six cannon.

The 2nd Hussars received three cannon as their share of the booty. Total British losses were 1,100 men; the 2nd Hussars lost one officer killed and one officer, thirty-two hussars and forty-six horses wounded.

Had La Peña acted, Victor's men must have been completely destroyed, but even after the victory he was so fearful that General Graham removed himself and his men from under his command and returned to Cadiz. The 2nd Hussars carried the battle honour 'Barossa' until after 1914.

Massena's Withdrawal

Defeated by the Lines of Torres Vedras, Masséna withdrew his scarecrow soldiers back into Spain in March 1811. Wellington followed and on 1 April he reached the River Coa, which here formed the border, where General Reynier stood to bar his further advance.

Here occurred the combat of Sabugal where Reynier was completely defeated and the 1st Hussars captured four officers, ninety men, ninety horses and twenty-five mules loaded with valuables.

By May 1811 Portugal was again clear of the enemy, except for the fortress of Almeida. Masséna concentrated his army about Ciudad Rodrigo and proceeded to feed and reorganize them. Since the day after the Battle of Busaco on 27 September 1810, Masséna had lost 30,000 men without fighting a battle; a few weeks' rest, and this energetic man again had an army of 40,000 infantry, 5,000 cavalry and thirty guns in a fit state to take up the offensive.

Wellington commanded 32,000 infantry, 1,500 cavalry and forty-two guns, and now set about recapturing Almeida. On 5 May the Battle of Fuentes de Oñoro occurred when Masséna tried to relieve Almeida. Of the Legion, the 1st Hussars, the 1st and 2nd Light Battalions and the 1st, 2nd, 5th and 7th Line Battalions were engaged; total Legion losses were eight officers and 147 men. The British lost 1,800 men. The French lost many more and were thrown back from Almeida, but General Brennier, commander of the French garrison, managed to break out and get his men safely through to Ciudad Rodrigo.

Masséna now withdrew to Salamanca, and Napoleon was so displeased that he recalled Masséna and replaced him with Marmont.

While Wellington was clearing north Portugal, Hill in the south was opposed by Soult's and Mortier's corps who intended to break into Portugal and join up with Masséna.

Badajoz was captured by the French on 10 March 1811 and the smaller Spanish fortresses of Olivenza and Campo Mayor fell soon afterwards.

Beresford now took over from Hill and, with reinforcements, he took up the offensive. With Beresford's force were the two Legion batteries of Cleeves (formerly von Rettberg) and Sympher, and on 17 April the 1st and 2nd Light Battalions of the Legion joined them.

After Soult had sent part of his Cadiz siege force to aid Masséna, Beresford took the opportunity to recapture Olivenza and then proceeded to lay siege to Badajoz. On 22 April Wellington arrived at the fortress but returned to the main army after reconnoitering the place. During May, Soult returned to Badajoz and Beresford lifted the siege and moved away to Albuera to offer him battle. On 16 May 1811 Beresford's Anglo-German-Portuguese-Spanish army of 27,000 infantry, 2,000 cavalry and thirty-eight guns clashed with Soult's 26,000 infantry, 4,500 cavalry and fifty-two guns in one of the bloodiest British battles of the Peninsular War. When the Polish lancers of Soult's army outflanked the British infantry and cut them down, they also caused the Legion artillery heavy losses, including capturing three of their cannon, two of which were later recovered.

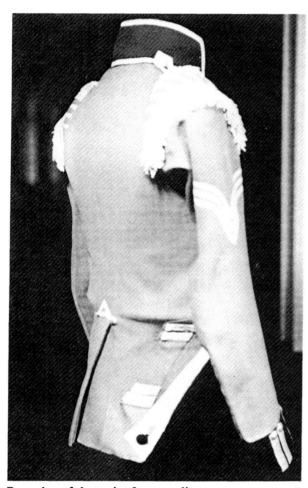

Rear view of the tunic of a grenadier company sergeant, K.G.L. line battalions, 1803–16. Although the buttons are missing from the lace on the false pocket flaps, this picture clearly shows the details of such tunics and settles the controversy as to whether the Legion had dark blue turnbacks (see Beamish, Schwertfeger, and subsequently Knötel) or white like their British comrades. The shoulder wings are also well illustrated. The grenade decoration on the white turnback has a dark blue body and a red flame. (Bomann Museum, Celle)

Finally the French withdrew but losses had been heavy: the two light battalions of the Legion lost eight officers and 105 men, the artillery batteries lost one officer, forty-eight men and thirty-six horses. Total Allied losses were about 6,000 men, the French about 7,000.

Beresford now handed over command to Hill, who took the army back to Badajoz and resumed the interrupted siege at the end of May. Due to the lack of experience of the British troops, the siege was not very actively pressed. Two attempts to storm the place failed and on 16 June the siege was broken off as Soult approached Badajoz with new forces.

At this point, three troops of the 2nd Hussars of the Legion joined Hill's corps and the two light battalions of the Legion were brigaded together with the Brunswick-Oels Jägers. The 7th Line Battalion was now so weak that it was decided to send the officers and N.C.O.s of the battalion back to England to recruit while the remaining men were split up among the other three battalions of the Legion with Hill's corps.

Hill now withdrew to the Portuguese fortress of Elvas. Soult and Marmont commanded 70,000 men at Badajoz while Wellington could raise only 50,000 to oppose them, but no great operations resulted and in July Soult moved off to the south to fight the Spanish, defeating them yet again on 9 August. Marmont moved up to Ciudad Rodrigo which Wellington was now menacing, in order to relieve that fortress. Marmont had 48,000 infantry, 6,000 cavalry and 100 guns.

Wellington's forces were quickly concentrated, and on 25 September 1811 occurred the clash at El Bodon in which the 1st Hussars of the Legion especially distinguished themselves against French cavalry three times as strong under General Montbrun. The 2nd Hussars lost forty-four men and fifty-two horses, the French many more. Wellington appeared and ordered a withdrawal, which was carried out in the best order for six miles under continual heavy enemy pressure.

The 1st Hussars wore the battle honour 'El Bodon' until the outbreak of the First World War.

Wellington's determined stance after this withdrawal deterred Marmont from battle and at the end of September he withdrew again. Wellington laid siege to Ciudad Rodrigo once more.

Meanwhile, in the south, Hill's corps (including a detachment of the 2nd Hussars of the Legion under Major von dem Busche) ambushed the French division of General Girard at Arroyo dos Molinos. Of the 2,500 infantry and 400 cavalry of Girard's division, 1,800 were killed, wounded or captured against an Allied loss of only seventy-two men. The 2nd Hussars captured ten officers and 200 men alone.

1812: Year of Victories

During the winter of 1811–12 Wellington prepared to bring the Siege of Ciudad Rodrigo to an end, and on 8 January 1812 he blockaded the place again. Of the Legion, the 1st, 2nd and 5th Line Battalions and Sympher's battery were present. The fortress was successfully stormed on 19 January, but although British losses were heavy (ninety officers and 1,200 men), the Legion got off lightly with two officers and eighty men as they were not involved in the final storming.

The speed of Wellington's action had completely surprised Marmont. After repairing the fortress and placing it under command of the Spanish General Castanos, Wellington moved against Badajoz.

During the winter Wellington had moved a siege-train up to Elvas, opposite Badajoz, in great secrecy and on 16 March 1812 Badajoz was blockaded by three British divisions. The Legion's units took no part in these siege operations. On 6 April the place was stormed and taken after bloody hand-to-hand fighting and then sacked by the British troops.

Losses were heavy; the Anglo-Portuguese Army had lost seventy-two officers and 963 men killed, and over 300 officers and 4,700 men wounded. The number of the garrison captured was less than the number of the Allied wounded.

Soult, who was still two days' march away, learned of the fall of Badajoz and returned to Seville, which had immediately been blockaded by a Spanish force after his departure.

Wellington's army was now joined by the 1st Hussars of the Legion from Ciudad Rodrigo and by the 1st and 2nd Heavy Dragoons from Ireland, each with about twenty-five officers and 500 men in three squadrons, formed into their own brigade under Major-General von Bock.

Even though Napoleon was now mounting his massive assault on Russia, there remained in Spain over 170,000 French (and Allied) soldiers: Soult in the south had 58,000; Marmont in Leon with 55,000; Suchet in the east with 40,000. The reserve armies of Jourdan and Souham in Castile numbered 25,000 men.

Wellington, firmly in command of both Spanish border fortresses, now decided to go over to the offensive and to clear Spain of the French even though his own army numbered only 44,000 men and sixty-four guns after Hill's corps in the south had been deducted.

On 13 June Wellington's army moved out of Ciudad Rodrigo towards Salamanca, where Marmont's army lay, but Marmont fell back over the Douro and until mid-July nothing of importance occurred.

Marmont now began to manœuvre to outflank Wellington, and on 22 July the famous Battle of Salamanca took place, in which Marmont was completely defeated, losing 7,000 prisoners, eleven guns, two eagles and eleven standards. Total Allied losses were 5,000 men; the Legion lost fifteen officers and 112 men dead and wounded. Sympher's battery had distinguished itself; the Hussars of the Legion had captured many prisoners as well as four guns and two standards.

Next day the chase was taken up, the foremost of Wellington's troops being the 1st and 2nd Light Battalions of the Legion. At Garcia Hernandez the French rearguard was encountered and the two heavy dragoon regiments of the Legion earned undying fame in their famous charge during which they broke three enemy squares (those of the 76e, 6e and 69e Ligne of Foy's division). Within forty minutes the invincible dragoons had broken three squares and captured 1,400 prisoners at a cost of six officers and 121 men killed or wounded (fifty-one were killed on the spot) and sixty-eight horses killed and seventy-two wounded.

Garcia Hernandez created such an impression on the British Government that all officers of the King's German Legion were accepted into the British Army as equals with their British comrades their seniority dating from the day their commissions had been issued.

Those Legion officers serving with acting rank were granted these ranks on a permanent basis. They also now had the right to a pension or 'half-pay' from the British Government.

The battle honour 'Garcia Hernandez' was carried by the 1st and 2nd Dragoons of the Legion until the First World War.

Marmont was pursued over the Douro and on 30 July Wellington was at Valladolid, but here he decided to turn east to drive King Joseph out of his capital at Madrid, leaving 18,000 men to watch Marmont's beaten army (which had now been taken over by Clausel).

On 11 August 1812, when the men of Wellington's army were enjoying a rest day, lancers of Berg and Italian dragoons of General Treilhard's brigade raided the cavalry lines, overthrew General d'Urban's young Portuguese cavalry brigade (which was the covering force) and broke in among the dragoons of the Legion. Luckily, the 1st Light Battalion of the Legion was also there and were able to fight for time to allow the dragoons to saddle up, mount and throw themselves at the attackers. Eventually General Ponsonby appeared with a British cavalry brigade and the assailants withdrew. The dragoons of the Legion had lost seven officers and forty-eight men dead and wounded. Wellington was so pleased with their conduct that he put them at the head of the column of Allied troops which entered Madrid on 12 August 1812.

The loss of the capital caused Soult to break off the siege of Cadiz, evacuate Andalusia and hurry to join King Joseph and Suchet in Murcia. Clausel had also now put his army into a battleworthy state and Wellington had to choose which of these gathering enemies to deal with before they united and destroyed him. He chose Clausel and, leaving a few divisions in Madrid under General Karl von Alten of the Legion, he marched north against the French-held town of Burgos which he reached on 19 September.

Burgos not only commanded the main route into France but was also a major depot of the French forces in Spain and thus of great importance. Wellington, however, had no siege-train with him.

With Wellington's force were the 1st, 2nd and 5th Line Battalions, while the 1st and 2nd Light Battalions were attached to the 7th Division on observation duties.

Burgos was stormed on the night of 22/23 September, but this attempt was repulsed as was a second attempt on 29 September. On 4 October the first of the triple ring of the defences was taken, during which action the Legion lost two officers and seventeen men dead or wounded out of a total engaged of sixty-two. The garrison of Burgos mounted raids on 5 and 8 October and the Legion battalions lost 135 officers and men killed and wounded.

A further attempt to storm the inner defences was bloodily repulsed on 18 October. To date,

Coat and shako of a sergeant of a line battalion, centre company, 1812–16. Note that the shoulder-strap is set slightly back on the shoulder. The cords on the 'Belgic' shako are incorrectly hung, and should be hooked to the right-hand side of the lower pat of the shako, just where it meets the higher front plate. (Bomann Museum, Celle)

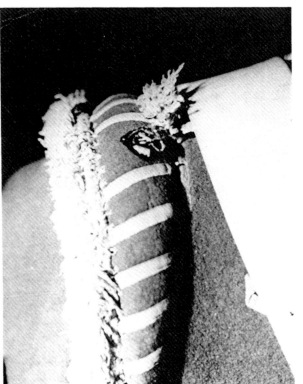

Detail of the wing on the tunic of a colour-sergeant, 7th Line Battalion, 1802–16. Note the interesting but as yet wholly unexplained badge worn on the wing by this man: a white thread bugle-horn embroidered on a tiny dark blue diamond-shaped patch. It is unique among the Bomann Museum uniforms, and is probably a 'domestic' battalion practice

Wellington's besieging force had lost over 2,000 men, the Legion nineteen officers and 349 men.

The concentration of French armies in his rear now forced Wellington to break off the Siege of Burgos and withdraw into Portugal.

He was followed by the French General Souham with 44,000 men who caught up with the British rearguard at Venta del Pozo on 23 October. In this rearguard were the two heavy dragoon regiments, the 1st Hussars and the two light battalions of the Legion.

Once again the enemy cavalry included the lancers of Berg and in the heavy cavalry battle which followed, the Legion dragoons lost nine officers and forty-seven men killed or wounded and thirty-nine men captured. Luckily they were taken up by the two light battalions who shattered the victorious enemy cavalry on their steady squares. As a mark of Wellington's esteem for their conduct, both battalions were later granted the battle honour 'Venta del Pozo' which was worn by their descendant battalions until the First World War.

Madrid also had to be evacuated and almost all the hard-won fruits of the 1812 campaign were lost. On 29 October 1812 Wellington's hard-pressed army crossed the Douro into Portugal again. During November Hill's corps joined him and brought the total Allied strength up to 68,000 men and seventy guns. They now went into winter quarters around Ciudad Rodrigo. The only remaining result of the 1812 campaign was that southern Spain remained free of the French and thus the Spanish Junta was at last able to reorganize its shattered armies.

During the winter the 2nd Hussars of the Legion was sent back to England to recruit and remount and thus the Legion cavalry in Portugal was reduced to the Heavy Dragoon Brigade and the 1st Hussars who were brigaded with the 18th British Hussars.

The two light battalions and the 1st, 2nd and 5th Line Battalions were brigaded under Major-General von Hinüber; as he was in Sicily at this point, Colonel Colin Halkett represented him.

The Legion Brigade and the Guards Brigade now formed the 1st Division of the army under General Sir Thomas Graham. General Karl von Alten of the Legion continued to command the Light Division which consisted of British and Portuguese troops.

Sympher's nine-pounder battery was with the field army, but the other two batteries were in Lisbon. Lieutenant-Colonel Hartmann of the Legion commanded Wellington's Reserve Artillery consisting of three British and one Portuguese battery.

1813: Into France

Marshal Soult was now recalled to Germany to take command of the Imperial Guard, and French forces in Spain were disposed as follows: King Joseph in Madrid, Castile and Navarre with over 100,000 men; Suchet in Valencia with 35,000 men; and a further 45,000 men were required for internal security duties.

Wellington could oppose this with an army of 70,000 men and 102 guns and had also the ubi-

16

quitous Spanish guerrillas who made the enemy's rear areas utterly unsafe. He was now also Generalissimo of the all-Spanish forces and could thus finally bring about some cohesion in the Allied operations in the Peninsula, including the movements of the 50,000-strong Spanish army.

An English landing on the east Spanish coast now cut Suchet's communications with France, and British naval support (a massive factor throughout the entire campaign) was readily available wherever required.

To the British raiding force under Murray on the eastern Spanish coast belonged the 4th and 6th Line Battalions and the sharpshooters detachments of the 3rd, 7th and 8th Line Battalions of the Legion as well as a small artillery detachment. From Alicante, Murray moved against Suchet in March 1813 with 16,000 men. There was a clash at Castalla (where the Legion lost three officers and fifty-five men) and Suchet was thrown back, but Murray also withdrew into Alicante. From here his corps was moved by sea to besiege Tarragona, but broke this operation off after only eight days. Murray was replaced by Lord Bentinck who then moved against Valencia in September, causing Suchet to withdraw into Catalonia and blew up Tarragona as he went.

In May 1813 General Graham with half Wellington's army was secretly sent over the Douro to advance to the Esla. With him he had the five battalions of the Legion and Hartmann's Reserve Artillery. General Hill took the rest of the army against Salamanca, thus threatening King Joseph's army from two sides. Joseph evacuated Salamanca and withdrew northwards. On 3 June the two halves of Wellington's army reunited in Toro and rushed after the enemy who, surprised by this speed, fell back over the Ebro and surrendered Burgos without a shot. There followed the Battle of Vittoria on 21 June 1813 – which decided the fate of the French control of Spain.

Joseph had 65,000 men on this battlefield, Wellington had 60,000 Anglo-German-Portuguese and 20,000 Spaniards.

Graham's corps undertook an outflanking movement to cut the French withdrawal route and the 2nd Light Battalion captured four cannon and a howitzer. Joseph could not now withdraw on Bayonne and had to flee to Pamplona, his army a disorganized rabble, without baggage or artillery. The French artillery losses at Vittoria were 150 pieces (they escaped with only one cannon and one howitzer and even these were lost the next day!).

Hartmann and his artillery had contributed greatly to the Allied victory; he set up a huge battery of forty-five guns in the centre of the line thus pioneering the massed artillery used by Napoleon at Waterloo in 1815. Legion losses were light; only the light battalions had been engaged.

Joseph's detached corps of Clausel (15,000 men) saved itself with difficulty and lost all its artillery, and that of General Foy (12,000 men) managed to withdraw from Bilbao to Bayonne and took up a position in Tolosa. General Graham drove him out of here on 23 June, whereby the Legion lost fourteen officers and 156 men. Hill's corps pushed towards Pamplona after the remnants of Joseph's army which they reached on 7 July.

The fortress of Pamplona was now blockaded by a Spanish force and Graham stood at San Sebastian – apart from these places Spain was at last clear of the enemy.

San Sebastian's garrison was 3,500 men under General Rey and he was soon to be supported by a new French field army of 80,000 men once again under Marshal Soult who had been expressly brought back from Germany to prop up France's sagging southern front.

On 25 July Soult advanced against Wellington to relieve Pamplona. He made some progress, but the arrival of Wellington with his troops restored the balance, and on 30 July the Allies went over to the offensive and threw the French back to their start positions.

Having neutralized Soult, Wellington returned to San Sebastian which was stormed and taken on 31 August, although the citadel held out until 8 September. During the siege the Legion had lost seventy men.

On 7 October Wellington crossed the Bidassoa, and his army entered France. Pamplona fell on 31 October and Wellington could now regroup his forces. On 10 November he forced the fortified line of the River Nivelle where the Legion losses were six officers and 153 men dead and wounded.

There followed the Battle of the River Nive from 10 to 13 December and then the unsuitable winter weather caused operations to be brought to an end.

Operations in Northern Europe

Three squadrons of the 3rd Hussars of the Legion were present during Graham's unfortunate Antwerp campaign of February 1814.

In the spring of 1813 the French were driven out of northern Hanover by the pursuing armies of the Russians; and Legion cadres were sent home to help organize the immediate mobilization of

Rear view of a dolman of an officer of the Horse Artillery of the Legion, in the Bomann Museum, Celle. Now faded to dark green, this garment was originally dark blue; the colour and cuffs are red, the lace and buttons gold. The front has three rows of buttons and seventeen rows of lace. The spherical buttons are stamped K over GL; the centre row are three-quarters of an inch in diameter, the outer rows half an inch. Gold Hungarian knots surmount the cuffs. The bandolier is covered in gold embroidery, and the black pouch bears the entwined cipher GR beneath a crown

the male population in the Allied cause. The French crushed this brief liberation, however, and operations during the spring and summer – interrupted by an armistice – ended with the French under Marshal Davout, and the Allies under Lieutenant-General Graf Wallmoden-Gimborn (son of the Hanoverian commander who had capitulated to the French at Artlenburg in 1803) eyeing each other from opposite banks of the Elbe, until Napoleon's abdication brought the war to an end.

Legion units involved in this campaign were initially four infantry companies, later reinforced and concentrated in a formation known as 'Holtzermann's Half-Battalion'. In the later stages of the fighting the remounted and 800-strong 3rd Hussars (Lieutenant-Colonel von Töbing, later Major Küper) and both horse artillery batteries also figured in the roll of Wallmoden's army. On 10 September 1813 Wallmoden fought a mismanaged action against the inferior French forces of General Pecheux at the Göhrde stream, and the Legion artillery and 3rd Hussars added this name to their battle honours. At Göhrde the Hussars lost eight officers, eighty-seven men and 146 mounts dead and wounded; the total Allied losses were thirty-two officers, 526 men and 306 horses, so the Legion's part is clear to see.

In December 1813 Wallmoden moved into Denmark, but received a sharp and costly rebuff at Sehestadt on the 10th of that month, at the hands of a Danish force under Prince Friedrich von Hessen. Captain Holtzermann was among the 600 captured. Wallmoden's forces later besieged Hamburg.

The Year 1814

At the end of 1813 the two regiments of heavy dragoons of the Legion were converted to light dragoons; their old brigade commander, General von Bock, was drowned in a shipwreck in the Bay of Biscay.

Wellington divided his army into three corps under Hill, Beresford and Hope; with the latter were the five infantry battalions of the Legion. They now formed one brigade commanded by

Major-General von Hinüber, and Lieutenant-Colonel von dem Busche commanded both light battalions. The dragoons and the 1st Hussars of the Legion formed part of the Cavalry Division under Cotton. Sympher's battery was with the 4th Division, and three ammunition columns were crewed by Legion gunners.

In mid-February Bayonne was placed under siege by General Hope's corps while Wellington's centre and right moved to manœuvre Soult out of his defensive line along the River Adour.

On 27 February Wellington defeated Soult at the Battle of Orthez at which Sympher's battery fought well although Major Sympher himself was killed, hit directly in the chest by a cannon-ball. Captain Daniel assumed command of the battery.

During the siege of Bayonne, which lasted until mid-April, Hill's corps caught up with part of Soult's army which was withdrawing after the Battle of Orthez, and defeated them again on 19 March; the dragoons of the Legion again distinguished themselves. The enemy fell back exposing Bordeaux, and Beresford marched on the town. The first Allied troops to enter Bordeaux were Captain Cordemann's squadron of the 1st Hussars of the Legion on 12 March 1814.

Soult meanwhile fell back on Tarbes and then Toulouse which he reached on 24 March. Wellington followed and on 10 April the Battle of Toulouse took place. The cavalry of the Legion overthrew a regiment of French hussars, capturing fifty and killing about the same number for the loss of five or six men. Daniel's battery of the Legion once again earned Wellington's praise for its cool conduct and accurate fire. The battle ended in a complete defeat for the French: total casualties on both sides were 6,500 men. Unfortunately, all this could have been avoided as Napoleon's fate was already sealed; on 31 March Paris had fallen but news of this reached Wellington only on 12 April.

At Bayonne, meanwhile, the French commander, although informed of the fall of Paris, refused to surrender and on 14 April the garrison made a rather pointless sortie, which caused heavy and unnecessary casualties to both sides. The losses of the 3rd Battalion of the Legion alone were fifteen officers and 145 men.

Bayonne capitulated on 28 April.

The End in the Mediterranean

On 9 March 1814 Lord William Bentinck landed in Livorno with a force of 8,000 men from Sicily. From the Legion the following units took part: 3rd, 6th and 8th Line Battalions under Major-Generals von Barsse and von Honstedt and a detachment of gunners from the 3rd Foot Battery. Captain Bindseil of the Legion artillery was in command of a British rocket battery. After the landing, Major-General von Barsse remained in Livorno as commandant while Bentinck took the main body of the force (now swollen to 15,000 men by Italian support) to Spezia. On 27 March Spezia was entered and Bentinck then proceeded along the coast to Genoa, which had a garrison of 6,000 men. A clash occurred at Genoa on 13 April in which the 8th Battalion of the Legion and the 31st (British) Foot figured well. German losses in the action were twenty-seven men.

Bentinck assaulted Genoa on 17 April with naval support; of the Legion only the 8th Battalion took part and had ten dead and forty-nine wounded; the 3rd and 6th Battalions were in the mountains on an outflanking movement and arrived at Genoa too late to fight. Genoa capitulated on 18 April 1814.

In the same month the 8th Line Battalion went to Corsica but did not come into action again; in May it sailed with the 3rd Battalion to Gibraltar. The 6th Battalion remained in Genoa.

The 7th Battalion and the 3rd Foot Battery were still in Sicily.

Quatre Bras

The units of the Legion engaged here were Major Kuhlmann's 2nd Horse Artillery Battery (which was attached to Major-General Cooke's First Division of the Prince of Orange's I Corps) and Captain Cleeve's nine-pounder foot battery, also attached to the 3rd Division of I Corps.

Kuhlmann's battery appeared on the battlefield with the 1st Division (which was composed of the British Foot Guards) at about four in the afternoon and was quickly brought into action by the farm at Quatre Bras. Cleeve's battery soon joined them. This was the time of the first heavy French cavalry attack, when Kellermann's cuirassiers, who had just successfully cut up the 3rd Hanoverian Brigade of Colonel Colin Halkett (the Legion officer who had been detached to the newly formed Hanoverian Landwehr), were advancing up the Brussels road on Quatre Bras. With a salvo of well-placed shots, the magnificent cuirassiers were thrown back in disarray and even Kellermann had to make his way to the rear on foot.

Shortly after this the Duke of Wellington ordered a general advance against Ney's men, and the French were pushed off the battlefield.

(This battle has been much more exhaustively described in my book *The Black Brunswickers*, (Osprey, 1973).

On hearing the news of the defeat of the Prussians at Ligny on 16 June, the Duke of Wellington withdrew his forces northwards from Quatre Bras to his previously chosen battlefield of Waterloo, where he planned to join forces with Blücher's Prussians and to put a stop to Napoleon's drive on Brussels.

During the withdrawal from Quatre Bras, the 3rd Light Cavalry Brigade of Major-General Sir William Dörnberg (which consisted of the 1st and 2nd Light Dragoons of the Legion under Lieutenant-Colonels Bülow and de Jonquieres, and the 23rd British Light Dragoons under Colonel the Earl of Portarlington) was part of the rearguard of the Anglo-Allied army. Also in the rearguard was the 2nd Hussars of the Legion under Lieutenant-Colonel Linsingen, which was in the 5th Cavalry Brigade of Major-General Sir Colquhoun Grant with the 15th and 7th British Hussars under Lieutenant-Colonel Dalrymple and Colonel Sir Edward Kerrison.

At Genappe, on the stream of the same name, these troops were drawn up in front of the town when the withdrawing picquet of the 18th (British) Hussars was driven back on the main body by three squadrons of French cavalry who were soon joined by horse artillery who rapidly opened fire on the British rearguard. The Earl of Uxbridge, commanding the Anglo-Allied cavalry, ordered the rearguard to fall back, and the French immediately rushed upon them, thinking to gain an easy victory. To check the French, the 18th

(British) Hussars charged; a violent thunderstorm and cloudburst had made the ground miry and slowed down the pace of all movements. No serious clash resulted, the French lancers seemed to have changed their minds as to the advisability of a serious contest at this point.

Rapidly the British cavalry withdrew through the defile of Genappe and took up position to the north of the town. Gradually the French cavalry occupied the town and their lancers appeared on the main road out of the town. Uxbridge, intent on delaying the French advance for as long as possible to give the main body of the Anglo-Allied army time to take up position at Waterloo undisturbed, sent the 7th (British) Hussars to charge them and the advance of the lancers was checked but no decisive result in anyone's favour could be achieved. The 7th were withdrawn, the French lancers charged after them in great elation but were totally overthrown by the 1st Life Guards. The Anglo-Allied rearguard then continued their withdrawal into the famous Waterloo position without further interference.

Just before twilight the 7th (British) Hussars and the Right Troop of the 2nd Light Dragoons of the Legion under Lieutenant Hugo, charged the French advanced guard near Mon Plaisir, drove them back and recaptured three carriages full of British sick and wounded.

The Legion at Waterloo

(It is not possible to include a full description of the field of Waterloo in this book.)

The continuous heavy rain of 17 June and the early morning of the 18th made Napoleon's attacks very tedious and exhausting affairs for the French and definitely contributed to the Anglo-Allied victory.

The deployment of the units of the King's German Legion on the field at the start of this day was, from east to west:

1 On the extreme left of the Allied first line - the 1st Hussars, as part of Vivian's Light Cavalry Brigade with the 10th and 18th (British) Hussars

2 In the centre of the Allied line, directly north of La Haye Sainte and across the line of the Genappe-Brussels road - the 2nd Brigade of th

Legion (part of Alten's 3rd Division) commanded by Colonel Ompteda: 1st and 2nd Light Battalions, 5th and 8th Line Battalions.

The 1st Light Battalion was formed in column of companies at quarter distance, left in front; it was just behind the crossroads. To its right stood the 5th Line Battalion, formed in column at quarter distance on one of its centre companies. Behind these two columns was the 8th Line Battalion, deployed as for the 5th. The 2nd Light Battalion occupied the farm of La Haye Sainte and put it into a fortified state.

3 On the right of the line, between Hougoumont and Merbe Braine – the 2nd Infantry Division (Major-General Sir Henry Clinton) consisting of the 3rd British Light Brigade and the 1st Brigade of the Legion under Colonel du Plat, and the 3rd Hanoverian Brigade.

Du Plat's brigade included the 1st, 2nd, 3rd and 4th Line Battalions, all in open column.

4 In the second Allied line, on the right and behind the crest of the hill on which Wellington had drawn up his army – the 3rd Cavalry Brigade (Major-General Sir William Dörnberg) including the 23rd (British) Light Dragoons and the 1st and 2nd Light Dragoons of the Legion.

5 To the left of the 3rd Cavalry Brigade and to the right rear of Alten's 3rd Division – the 3rd Hussars of the Legion under Colonel Sir Frederick von Arentsschildt.

6 *The artillery.* Immediately to the west and north of La Haye Sainte was the foot battery of Captain Cleeve (together with the British battery of Major Lloyd). The 1st Horse Battery of the Legion, under Major Kuhlmann, was in the angle between the roads from Mont St Jean to Nivelles and from La Haye Sainte to Braine le Allaud, west of the crossing-point of these roads. The 2nd Horse Battery of Major Sympher was next to and due east of Du Plat's brigade.

As has previously been mentioned, the ground between the opposing armies at Waterloo was very soft and miry after the rain, and this probably accounted for Napoleon's delayed attacks on 18 June in that he wished to give the soil a chance to dry out and thus make movements easier.

At this point, the Legion strength on the field was 3,301 infantry, 1,991 cavalry and 526 artillery with eighteen guns in three batteries.

The first shots of the battle were fired at about 11.30 a.m. when French skirmishers began to close in on the tactically important farm of Hougoumont which was held by the British Guards. Soon a column from Prince Jerome's division of Reille's corps was seen coming up behind these skirmishers and Wellington ordered Captain Sandham's British battery and Captain Cleeve's battery of the Legion to shell it, which they did with good effect.

Later, as Jerome stiffened his assault on Hougoumont and Pire's cavalry guns came into play, Major Sympher's 2nd Horse Artillery Battery of the Legion was also brought into action against them.

The action had become general now along the whole line: at 1 p.m. the dark mass of Bülow's Prussian corps had been seen by Napoleon in the

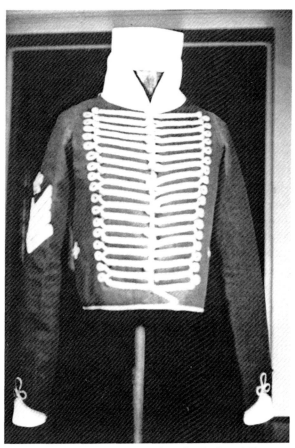

Dolman of a sergeant-major of the Legion's 3rd Hussars, 1813–16. This traditional hussar garment originated in Hungary, as did its wearer. Note the peculiar cut at the bottom of the front of the dolman. Facings are edged with silver lace, as are the yellow rank chevrons, and the lace and buttons on the front are silver. (Bomann Museum, Celle)

Detail of the parade uniform of an officer of the centre companies of the 1st Line Battalion, 1803–16. **This uniform is displayed in the Bomann Museum; it has a gilt gorget inscribed GR, but the author is unaware of any contemporary plates confirming this**

distance approaching at St Lambert, and shortly after this D'Erlon's corps had attacked the extreme left of the Allied line (Prince Bernhard of Saxe-Weimar's Nassauers and Dutch-Belgians). The Allied troops, exposed to the fire of seventy-four French cannon and suffering heavily from them, were driven out of the farm of Papelotte and fell back to the rear, past the British troops of Picton's division. This left Picton facing assaulting French columns four times the strength of his own formation, many of whose regiments had lost up to half their strength at Quatre Bras on 16 June. Nothing daunted, Picton let the French close to 'eyeball' distance, gave them a devastating volley and chased them back down into the valley. Unfortunately, in this moment of victory, Picton was killed by a musket ball in the head.

Kempt's brigade of Picton's division was supported in this glorious charge by the 1st Light Battalion of the Legion under Colonel von dem Busche.

Just at the end of this exciting episode, Donzelot's division advanced against La Haye Sainte, held by six companies of the 2nd Light Battalion of the Legion under Major Baring, supported by two companies of the 1st Light Battalion and a company of Hanoverian riflemen (under Major Sporken). Initially, Baring had occupied the orchard as well as the buildings of the place but the heavy French pressure made him withdraw into the barn. Wellington, seeing the precarious state of Baring's little garrison, ordered the Lüneburg Field Battalion of Kielmannsegge's Hanoverian brigade to reinforce him.

Baring counter-attacked to regain the orchard but the newly arrived Hanoverians became confused, were ridden over by French cuirassiers and fell back to the main Allied position, suffering heavy loss from cavalry and flanking enemy fire on the way. Part of this unit remained in La Haye Sainte with Baring's men for the rest of that day. These events were followed by the famous Union Brigade charge during which Sergeant Ewart of the Royal North British Dragoons (Scots Greys) captured the eagle of the 45th French Line Infantry Regiment, and Captain Clark of the 1st Royal Dragoons took the eagle of the 105th French Line Infantry Regiment.

It was now about 3 p.m. and Bachelu's division advanced against La Haye Sainte, which was still holding out in stubborn fashion after defeating D'Erlon's attack.

Bachelu's column had inclined slightly towards Hougoumont when Captain Cleeve's foot battery of the Legion poured three rounds from each gun into it at close range and sent the survivors of the carnage rushing back to shelter. Bachelu rallied his men and advanced again only to be dealt with once more in the same manner, and an apparent flank attack on Hougoumont was thus foiled by the fire of a single battery.

Major Baring in La Haye Sainte meanwhile was being hard pressed and asked for reinforcements; he was sent two companies of the 1st Light Battalion of the Legion and they helped to stave off the furious French assaults on the buildings (which was all that Baring still controlled of the farm).

Due to the heavy fighting Baring was now running short of ammunition, but although he twice sent requests for resupply none came. It was this fact which eventually led to the evacuation of La Haye Sainte later in the day. At about 5 p.m. the cavalry of the Imperial Guard were assaulting the right of the Allied line and, when they fell back, the 1st Light Dragoons of the Legion pursued the Red Lancers back to their lines, only to be chased away in their turn. The 1st Light Dragoons of the Legion, the 7th British Hussars and the Brunswick Hussars (with their Lancer Squadron) were the only Allied cavalry on the right of the line at this time.

The repeated French cavalry attacks, unsupported by infantry, were without serious effect on Wellington's men and, indeed, provided a welcome respite from the bombardment of Napoleon's great artillery battery which played on the Allied line until their own cavalry closed with the Anglo-Allied troops.

French lancers once again attacked the right of Wellington's line and were charged by the heavily outnumbered 1st Light Dragoons of the Legion and thrown back.

Du Plat's brigade (5th and 8th Line Battalions of the Legion) was ordered to advance against the French forces assaulting La Haye Sainte. In the movement over the fire-swept ground, every mounted officer of the brigade had his horse shot from under him, and Du Plat himself was killed. Colonel Ompteda assumed command of the brigade and led them forward against the enemy.

Unfortunately, at this point the Chasseurs of the Imperial Guard, having just been thrown back from an unsuccessful attack on Kielmannsegge's Hanoverian brigade up on the crest of the ridge which formed the Allied position, rode back down the slope towards their own position and thus into the rear of Ompteda's brigade.

The 5th Battalion saw the danger and were able to form square in time, but the 8th Battalion was completely surprised, taken in line in rear and scattered. Ensign von Moreau, who was carrying the King's Colour of the 8th Battalion, was badly wounded and gave the flag to his colour-sergeant who, however, was also wounded. The French captain who took the colour was killed immediately but the flag remained in French hands during the rest of the battle.

Some days after the action the flag was returned to the battalion by a Hanoverian cavalryman.

For the remainder of the day of 18 June, the remnants of the 8th Battalion were drawn up into a square under command of Major von Petersdorff.

La Haye Sainte was still being heavily contested and Major Baring now sent a second urgent message for ammunition resupply – again without success – but the light company of the 5th Line Battalion of the Legion was sent to reinforce him and in another forty minutes the two flank companies of the 1st Regiment of Nassau also joined him.

During the previous night the door of the barn had been broken up for firewood and the resulting hole had been hotly contested for hours. Now fire broke out, but the garrison put it out with water taken from the farm pond by the men in their camp kettles and even their shakos.

The Fall of La Haye Sainte

As already mentioned, Baring had now twice asked urgently for ammunition for his small garrison but had received none. After using up all the cartridges on the dead and wounded, the fire of the Germans and Nassauers against the continuous French assaults slackened and finally stopped altogether. At last the French could make headway into the burning farm and Baring and his small garrison had to withdraw up the hill to the main Anglo-Allied line and joined up with two companies of the 1st Light Battalion of the Legion. It was now half-past six o'clock and the battle for La Haye Sainte had raged since half-past one.

A further French column of assault now appeared near La Haye Sainte and the Prince of Orange ordered the 5th Line Battalion of the Legion to advance in line and attack it, thus committing his second serious mistake of the Waterloo campaign (his first had been at Quatre Bras when he countermanded Halkett's orders for the 69th Regiment to form square to receive cavalry and thus caused that regiment to be badly cut up).

The mistake of the Prince of Orange was that

he twice ignored the advice of Colonel Ompteda, commander of the 5th Line Battalion, who pointed out to the rash young prince that French cuirassiers were lurking in a hollow ahead and that to advance in line, without any cavalry protection, would be suicide. The Prince of Orange would hear none of this and, with the fateful self-confidence of military ignorance, impatiently insisted that his orders should be carried out.

With exemplary self-control and self-discipline, Ompteda replied, 'Well, I will!' drew his sword and led his 'Fighting Battalion', as it was called, forward. He then asked Lieutenant-Colonel von Linsingen to try and save his two fifteen-year-old nephews who were serving as ensigns in the 5th Battalion, and rode on. At this point the 5th Battalion was only about 200 bayonets strong, but they charged forward with their accustomed vigour and were taken in the right flank by the waiting cuirassiers and cut down. Colonel Ompteda was last seen, way ahead of his men, cutting through a column of French infantry. His body was later recovered. Lieutenant-Colonel von Linsingen's horse was shot from under him and he lay pinned under the dead animal for some time. Finally, he extricated himself, saw that his battalion had been destroyed, grasped Ompteda's two young nephews by their shoulder-wings and dragged them into safety in a ditch.

The 5th Line Battalion was now reduced to six officers and eighteen unwounded men; five officers, 130 N.C.O.s and men had been killed or badly wounded in this unnecessary tragedy and the remainder of the men were missing.

The loss of La Haye Sainte and the destruction of the 5th Battalion of the Legion made Wellington's left flank very vulnerable.

The brigades of Pack, Kempt, Lambert, Best and Vincke were still in position on the ridge but were considerably weakened by losses, and the village of Papelotte had had to be evacuated by its garrison of Nassauers. Ammunition was running low, many guns now had no teams to move them or were damaged, and cavalry strength along the whole line was pitifully reduced.

General Karl von Alten and the Prince of Orange had both been wounded and both had been forced to leave the field (although in the case of the latter this may have been regarded as a blessing in disguise!).

Unfortunately, at this critical time, one of the newly formed Hanoverian cavalry regiments, the Cumberland Hussars, calmly walked off the battlefield towards Brussels in spite of all that was said to persuade them to stay. Their commander, Colonel Hake, was later cashiered for this extraordinary conduct.

Morale began to sag in the Anglo-Allied line as it was observed that the French were preparing for yet another massive assault, and an ominous sign was that many regiments sent their colours to the rear.

It was at this point that Wellington, having ordered all units to stand fast and fight to the last man, uttered his famous phrase, 'Night or the Prussians must come.'

As if in answer to his prayers, effective Prussian forces were now disputing possession of Plancenoit with the Imperial Guard (on Napoleon's right

Detail of the turnbacks of an officer's coat, 1st Line Battalion, centre companies. The long skirts of the parade coat have white turnbacks decorated with dark blue velvet diamonds bearing in silver K.G.L. beneath a crown and above crossed branches. The patch has a silver embroidered edge. (Bomann Museum, Celle)

1 Corporal, 1st Heavy Dragoons,
parade dress, 1808–13
2 Officer, 2nd Heavy Dragoons,
campaign dress, Spain 1812
3 Trooper, 3rd Light Dragoons,
parade dress, 1809

Michael Roffe

1 Trooper, 2nd Light Dragoons,
 field service dress, 1814–16
2 Officer, 1st Hussars, parade dress,
 1813–16
3 Officer, 2nd Hussars, parade dress,
 1813–16

B

Michael Roffe

1 Officer, Foot Artillery, parade dress,
  1812–16
2 Officer, 1st Light Battalion, field
  service uniform, 1808–16
3 Drummer, Foot Artillery, 1812–16

Michael Roffe

C

1 Rifleman, 2nd Light Battalion, field service marching order, 1815
2 Private, centre companies, line infantry battalions, parade dress, 1803–08
3 Private, centre companies, line battalions, field service marching order, 1812–16

Michael Roffe

1 Bugler of Sharpshooters, line
battalions, field service marching
order, 1812–16
2 Sergeant-major, line battalions,
parade dress, 1812–16
3 Colour-bearer, 5th line battalion,
parade dress, 1815–16

Michael Roffe

E

Officer, Horse Artillery
parade dress, 1808–16

F

Michael Roffe

1 Trooper, 3rd Hussars, parade dress,
  1813–16
2 Janissary, 1st Light Battalion,
  parade dress
3 Mounted Gunner, Horse Artillery,
  field dress, 1808–16

Michael Roffe

G

1 Officer of Sharpshooters, line
  battalions, parade dress, 1812–16
2 Corporal of Sharpshooters, line
  battalions, skirmishing order,
  1812–16
3 Sergeant, light battalions, 'undress'
  walking-out dress, 1808–16

H

rear flank) and soon distracted Napoleon from his assaults on the dangerously weakened Anglo-Allied line. This was not yet the direct support which Wellington needed, but at about six o'clock Zieten's Prussian corps entered Ohain (about five kilometres east from Mont St Jean) and assaulted the French in the village of Papelotte which the French had recently taken from the Nassauers.

Wellington could now draw off forces from his left flank to prop up his centre and thus the two fresh cavalry brigades of Vandeleur and Vivian (including the 1st Hussars of the Legion) and Vincke's Hanoverian infantry brigade were transferred to the centre as were (from the left flank) the Brunswickers and Chassé's Dutch-Belgian infantry division together with the 1st Light Dragoons of the Legion who had been transferred to this point during the afternoon.

Now Wellington had secured the shaky centre of his line and when Napoleon made his last desperate attack with the apparently invincible Imperial Guard at about quarter-past seven, Wellington was able to beat off the assault with Maitland's, Adam's and Byng's brigades.

As soon as it became apparent that the Imperial Guard had been defeated, the fight went out of the majority of Napoleon's army like the air out of a burst balloon. They fell back on all fronts, the confusion and lack of discipline increasing with every minute.

Wellington now gave the signal for a general advance by waving his hat and the whole line rolled forward down the hill after the fleeing French.

Only the brigades of Pack, Ompteda, Kielmannsegge and some immobilized artillery batteries remained on the crest of the hill which had been so desperately fought over all day.

It was now quarter-past eight.

Vivian's and Vandeleur's cavalry brigades (including the 1st Hussars of the Legion) raced ahead of their comrades and hacked their way through the demoralized French fugitives with the wild battle cry of 'No quarter!' Their bloody progress continued until they were brought up by the still-intact squares of the Imperial Guard which Napoleon had formed in order to permit an orderly withdrawal to be organized.

The advance of Blücher's Prussians out of Plancenoit, however, destroyed this hope and the vast majority of the French Army dissolved into a rabble, each seeking to save himself. At quarter-past nine that night Wellington and Blücher met at La Belle Alliance and Wellington entrusted the pursuit of the beaten French to the Prussians – his own men, having fought for ten hours, were too exhausted to march far. Only the Hanoverian Landwehr Battalion Osnabrück, commanded by Colonel Hugh Halkett, took part in the further pursuit as far as Genappe, and Colonel Halkett captured the French General Comte Cambronne of the Imperial Guard, dragging him off to captivity by his aiguillette.

The Disbanding of the Legion

In December 1815 it was decided that the King's German Legion was to march from Paris to Hanover in order to be disbanded there, the majority of the officers and men to be taken into the newly re-formed Hanoverian Army.

By 24 February 1816 the 1st, 2nd, 3rd, 4th, 5th and 8th Battalions had been disbanded in and around Osnabrück and their flags were laid up with great ceremony in the old garrison church, where they remained until 1867 (when Prussia annexed Hanover).

The five cavalry regiments and the artillery were also disbanded on this day, the 1st Hussars and some artillery being the only units to enjoy the privilege of a ceremonial entry into the town of Hanover; the Hussars were followed by three batteries of Legion artillery and one of Hanoverian and twenty captured cannon.

The 6th and 7th Battalions and the 3rd Foot Battery were still in the Mediterranean and did not return to Hanover until April 1816 when they were disbanded and reorganized.

In 1867 the Hanoverian Army was disbanded (after winning the Battle of Langensalza against the Prussians) but on 24 January 1899 the Prussian Emperor ordered that the traditions of the units of the King's German Legion were to be taken up by the Hanoverian units of the Prussian Army. This continued until the First World War.

Legion units	1816 (Hanoverian Army)	1914 (Prussian Army)
1st Light Dragoons	Garde-Reuter-Regiment	Königs-Ulanen-Regiment (1. Hannoversches) Nr 13
2nd Light Dragoons	2. or Leib-Reuter-Regiment	2. Hannoversches Ulanen-Regiment Nr 14
1st Hussars	1. or Garde-Husaren-Regiment	Husaren-Regiment, Königin Wilhelmina der Niederlande (Hannoversches) Nr 15
2nd Hussars	2. or Osnabrücksches Husaren-Regiment	
3rd Hussars	3. or Göttingensches Husaren-Regiment	Dragoner-Regiment, König Carl I von Rumanien (1. Hannoversches) Nr 9
Artillery and Engineers	Artillerie- and Ingenieurcorps	Feldartillerie-Regiment von Scharnhorst (1. Hannoversches) Nr 10
		Hannoversches Pionier-Bataillon Nr 10
1st Light Battalion	Garde-Jäger-Bataillon	Hannoversches Jäger-Bataillon Nr 10
2nd Light Battalion		
3rd Line Battalion	2. Garde-Bataillon	
4th Line Battalion		
1st Line Battalion	1. Grenadier-Garde-Bataillon	Füsilier-Regiment Prinz Albert von Preussen (Hannoversches) Nr 73
2nd Line Battalion		
5th Line Battalion	3. Garde-Bataillon	
8th Line Battalion		
6th Line Battalion	Landwehr-Bataillone	
7th Line Battalion	Emden, Leer and Aurich	

The Organization of the Legion

ARTILLERY

The regimental staff: one colonel commander, one lieutenant-colonel, two majors, two adjutants, one quartermaster (Q.M.), one paymaster, five surgeons, one veterinary surgeon.

The junior staff: one sergeant-major, one quartermaster-sergeant (R.Q.M.S.), one paymaster-sergeant.

Apart from these there were the captain commissary and the school-master (for the soldiers' children).

Each horse artillery battery had: one captain 1st Class, one captain 2nd Class, two lieutenants, two second lieutenants, one battery sergeant-major (B.S.M.), one battery quartermaster-sergeant (B.Q.M.S.), three sergeants, four corporals, seven bombardiers, one trumpeter, ninety gunners, one farrier, two blacksmiths, two collar-makers (for repairing harness), two wheelwrights.

Then there was the train of: one sergeant, two corporals, one trumpeter, fifty-seven drivers.

The artillery pieces in each horse artillery battery were: five six-pounder cannon each drawn by six horses; one five-and-a-half-inch howitzer drawn by eight horses.

The foot batteries (both six- and nine-pounder) had the same six officers as the horse batteries but only three sergeants and, as long as the battery was static, two drummers who converted to mounted trumpeters when the battery was on the move.

Other mounted personnel were the officers, six non-commissioned officers, the train and the blacksmith.

The foot batteries had four guns and two five-and-a-half-inch howitzers and the nine-pounder battery was stronger than the six-pounder by three bombardiers, four gunners, thirty-nine drivers and one blacksmith. It also had four guns and two five-and-a-half-inch howitzers.

Ammunition wagons and the smith's field forge were drawn by six horses each, the other vehicles by four horses and the reserve gun carriages by two horses.

Each battery had eight ammunition wagons, two baggage wagons and one field forge. In addition there was a further wagon of small-arms ammunition and the reserve horses.

The gun carriages were lighter than those of the rest of the British Army and thus more manoeuvrable which was a considerable advantage in the Peninsular campaign.

The limbers initially were two-wheelers with seats on for the unmounted members of the battery, but in 1807 they were replaced by limbers of a type which also towed the gun and seats were also provided on these.

CAVALRY

A regiment consisted of: one colonel commander, two majors (one of which became a lieutenant-colonel), one adjutant, one paymaster, three surgeons, one veterinary surgeon, one regimental sergeant-major (R.S.M.), one paymaster-sergeant one saddler, one armourer, one farrier.

Each troop contained: one captain, one lieutenant, one cornet, one quartermaster, four sergeants, four corporals, one trumpeter, seventy-six troopers.

On 24 June 1809 a quartermaster of officer's rank was introduced for the whole regiment and the non-commissioned troop Q.M.s were abolished.

The troops were distinguished by the letters A, B, C, etc., and the squadrons by numbers 1–5. The troops and squadrons were organized as follows:

1 Squadron – A and F Troops
2 Squadron – B and G Troops
3 Squadron – C and H Troops
4 Squadron – D and I Troops
5 Squadron – E and K Troops

INFANTRY

Regimental staff (the term 'regiment' was used even though it was in fact a battalion): one colonel commander, one lieutenant-colonel, two majors, one adjutant, one auditor, one quartermaster, three surgeons, one R.S.M., one regimental auditor sergeant, one R.Q.M.S., one armourer.

Each company consisted of: one captain, two lieutenants, one ensign, five sergeants, five corporals (one of which was the company quartermaster), one drummer/bugler (line/light battalion), ninety-six privates (two of whom were drummers/trumpeters), one pioneer.

The companies were distinguished alphabetically within each battalion.

THE GARRISON COMPANY
(25 March 1805)

One captain, two lieutenants, one ensign, five sergeants, five corporals, two drummers, ninety-five privates. In December 1806 this was reduced to: one lieutenant, one sergeant, two corporals, forty-eight privates.

HORSES

Dragoons' horses were from fourteen hands one inch to sixteen hands two inches tall; hussars' horses were from fourteen hands one inch to fifteen hands two inches. (Nowadays, horses below fourteen hands two inches high are considered to be 'ponies'.)

Price limits for buying dragoon and hussar mounts were thirty guineas and twenty-five guineas respectively.

Colouring was mixed, but greys were used only by the musicians and trumpeters.

Tails were cropped as was the English fashion of the day and each horse had a name beginning with the initial letter of the troop to which it belonged.

TRAINING

The German officers, then as now, had a much more earnest approach to soldiering than their English counterparts and the standard of training of the King's German Legion was considerably higher than that of normal English line regiments. For example, in the Legion, the officers used to drill their men; a task left to their N.C.O.s by most English officers.

Initially, drill and commands were on the old Hanoverian model, and German was used. English superseded this in the artillery and cavalry in 1807, later than in the line battalions. The two light battalions retained their German customs to the end, but English drill was used in parades and guard mounting.

The Legion also absorbed many English sports such as cricket, football, boxing, rowing, quarterstaff fighting, etc. The officers adopted the English custom of foxhunting which they also enjoyed during the Peninsular campaign.

TACTICAL CAVALRY FORMATIONS

Cavalry formed in two ranks with four feet distance between them. The squadron was divided into four divisions and was commanded by the senior captain. Each lieutenant commanded a troop and positioned himself on the outer wing. The cornets were in the centre of the squadron. All officers were shadowed by N.C.O.s who took their places in their absence.

The second captain and the senior cornet commanded in the centre of the second rank.

The march was mostly at the trot, the charge at the gallop with four paces distance between ranks.

Skirmishers pushed out 300–400 paces from the main body at twenty-five-pace intervals along the front. In this formation the second rank of the main body were ten paces behind and to the left of the first.

When engaging the enemy, the first rank would have their sabres hanging from the sword-knots on their wrists and would engage the enemy with pistol or carbine according to range; the second rank drew and held only their sabres.

TACTICAL INFANTRY FORMATIONS

Companies consisted of two platoons each of two sections and were arranged in line precedence (according to the seniority of their officers) from right to left. With the introduction of ten companies per battalion in 1812 (including a grenadier and a light company), this system became inoperative as the grenadier company was always on the right and the light company always on the left of the battalion line.

Sharpshooters (a Hanoverian custom) were used in front of the battalion when in action. These sharpshooters were picked marksmen who carried rifles and wore distinguishing items of uniform. (See Colour Plates.)

They consisted of a subaltern, four sergeants, a bugler and fifty-two men per battalion. In action they formed into two detachments on the flanks and to the rear of the main body of the battalion. Sometimes all sharpshooters of a brigade would be collected together under a captain.

Left: Marshal Soult, Duc de Dalmatie or to English soldiers, 'The Duke of Damnation'! He was driven out of Oporto in May 1809 by Wellesley's army, which included 3,300 foot, horse and artillery of the Legion. His main area of operations during the Peninsular War was Andalusia in the south; after the fiasco of Vittoria, Napoleon put him in command of the French armies contesting Wellington's position in the Pyrenees

Centre: Murat, King of Naples: in September 1810 the 3rd, 4th and 6th Line Battalions of the Legion distinguished themselves in the repulse of his invasion of Sicily

Right: Marshal Masséna, for a long time the luckiest and most consistently successful of Napoleon's marshals, who failed conspicuously at Busaco and before the Lines of Torres Vedras. His subsequent retreat with his starving and ragged Army of Portugal was a harrowing experience for Allies and French alike

This policy was sometimes applied to the light companies as well, but very rarely to the grenadier companies.

The battle line was a double rank (since 1804) with two feet six inches distance between ranks; in order to fire, the second rank moved six inches forwards and to the right, thus moving into the spaces between their comrades in the front rank.

On parade the battalion commander and the adjutants were in the front centre of the battalion, captains on the right wings of their companies, other officers three paces to the rear of the second rank.

The famous square (a formation used to guard against attack by cavalry) was hollow and of three or four ranks' depth along each face; the outer two ranks would kneel.

Bayonets were normally carried fixed by the line battalions, but the light battalions only fixed them when specifically ordered.

Before closing with the enemy a salvo would be fired; line battalions then attacked at a speed of seventy-five paces to the minute and light batta-lions at 108 paces. On the command 'Charge' the first rank went into the 'on guard' position and the second rank shouldered arms, a 'Hurrah' was given and contact made.

Movements were mostly made in open columns of divisions, but closed column was used in action.

Column marches were carried out in four ranks but in Spain the narrow tracks forced the use of a three-abreast formation.

When fire-fighting with the enemy, the second rank would move forward past the first rank to fire and then retire again to load. Signals were given by whistle.

On parades and reviews a march past at seventy-five paces per minute was first performed with all officers dismounted; a second march past in quick time with officers mounted then followed. Officers saluted with the drawn sword only when mounted, but with drawn sword and by raising the left hand to the head-dress when on foot. (When mounted they required their left hands to hold the reins of their horses.) Other ranks always carried their arms shouldered.

Uniforms

Apart from minor appointments, the Legion was dressed exactly as were their British counterparts. These minor differences consisted of various initials and titles worn on cap-plates, belt-plates, buttons, turnbacks, packs and canteens.

Knötel, in his plate 24, Volume III of the series *Uniformenkunde*, shows the line battalions of the Legion with blue turnbacks to the skirts of their jackets and blue fields to the wings of the flank companies. In the notes to this plate Knötel states that in Beamish and von Brandis the turnbacks are white as for the British line infantry but that he has shown them blue because they appear so in *Costumes of the Army of the British Empire 1814*.

All the Legion line infantry jackets in the Bomann Museum in Celle and in the Hanover Museum show white turnbacks and *Costumes of the British Empire 1814* is the only source which the author knows which differs.

It has not been possible for the author to find a picture of the Legion infantry in the 'stovepipe' shako which was worn in the British Army from 1800 to 1812. The sketch in this book is therefore to be regarded as not absolutely reliable.

Coats of generals, staff officers, engineers and line infantry officers were long skirted (changed to short skirted in 1812). Other ranks' coats were always short skirted.

Facing colours on collars, cuffs and officers' lapels were dark blue for line infantry officers, black for engineers. Turnbacks were white for staff officers, generals and officers of the line battalions; collars and cuffs were blue.

Artillery coats were initially a short-skirted dark blue coat with red collar, cuffs and turnbacks. Later, however, the mounted batteries of the Legion adopted the blue dolman which the Royal Horse Artillery also had (and retain for ceremonial wear for King's Troop, R.H.A., to this day).

Heavy dragoon regiments. Scarlet coat with long skirts initially, later short. Facings on collar, cuffs and turnbacks: 1st Regiment – dark blue, 2nd Regiment – black. Lace and buttons were yellow.

On 25 December 1813 they became light dragoon regiments wearing dark blue kolletts with red lapels, cuffs, turnbacks and collars. Other ranks only received this uniform for the 1815 campaign.

Hussars. The 1st Regiment wore the same uniform as the old 9th Hanoverian Cavalry Regiment of 1803: a blue kollett with red facings and yellow lace and buttons. The other two regiments wore the normal British light dragoon uniform which later was of the hussar type. Initially they wore only a dolman, but the 3rd regiment wore red-lined pelisses from their formation and the other two regiments soon imitated them.

Facings: 1st Regiment – scarlet collar and cuffs; yellow lace and buttons.
         2nd Regiment – white collar and cuffs; yellow lace and buttons.
         3rd Regiment – yellow collar and cuffs; white lace and buttons.

Fur on the pelisses was black for the 1st Regiment, white for the 2nd and in the 3rd Regiment Knötel shows an officer in black fur and a hussar in grey in 1813.

The light battalions had a far more individual-

The French equivalent of the King's German Legion was the Légion Hanovrienne, which also fought in Spain until disbanded in 1811. The Legion reached a strength of two infantry battalions and two squadrons of *chasseurs à cheval*. They wore French-style uniforms, the coat being red, faced dark blue, with white buttons. The grenadier companies wore bearskin bonnets with red plumes and, it seems, white epaulettes; the voltigeurs wore the shako of the four centre companies but with green cords and plume, and also had green epaulettes. The *chasseurs* had dark green coats, faced yellow

istic uniform: the 1st Battalion had lighter green uniforms than the 2nd, collars and cuffs were black for both, but uniform cut varied also. The 1st Battalion had a jacket with very short skirts, whereas the 2nd Battalion wore a dolman (officers had black silk lacing on the chest which O.R.s did not have) with three rows of buttons.

Generals, and line battalion officers' coats were double breasted; the men's single breasted.

Button designs included the King's cipher, a crown, crossed sabres, a bugle, the name of the Legion in a garter form or the initials of the unit without the garter.

Buttons were gold for generals, the staff, engineers, artillery, both the Heavy and the 1st Light Dragoons and the line battalions; white for the 3rd Hussars and the light battalions.

Gold embroidery was sewn on to the collars, cuffs and breasts of the jackets of the generals, the staff and officers of engineers, artillery, heavy dragoons and infantry. The men's jackets were bordered with a white lace. Headgear was, for officers, mostly the black bicorne with black cockade and white-over-red plume. This was worn sideways in peacetime, but in action worn fore and aft and with brass chin scales. The tips of the bicorne almost reached the wearer's shoulders.

In 1811 the shako was introduced for officers of the foot artillery batteries, while the horse artillery officers wore the crested British light dragoon helmet.

The officers and men of the heavy dragoons wore iron cross-pieces under their bicornes in action; these metal skull-guards were called 'secrets'.

As from March 1812, line infantry officers adopted the '1812' pattern (or Waterloo pattern) shako for duty wear. The light dragoons also wore a shako (but of different pattern from the infantry) on their conversion from heavy dragoons, and the 1st and 2nd Hussars initially wore this headgear also, but the 3rd Regiment wore a busby of black fur with a red bag. This was rapidly copied by the other two regiments.

All ranks of the 1st Light Battalion wore a black conical shako, and officers of the 2nd a 'Winged cap' ('Flügelmütze' or 'Mirliton'), while the men wore the conical shako.

Generals and staff officers wore white breeches and hessian boots with spurs screwed in. Engineer officers wore grey trousers with a gold stripe; foot artillery officers grey with a red stripe; and O.R.s of foot artillery grey trousers without stripes, black lace shoes and black leather gaiters into which the trousers were sometimes put. Horse artillery on parade wore white breeches and hessian boots with buckle-on spurs, while the heavy dragoons wore the higher, cuffed boots and white breeches.

The 1st Hussars wore blue overalls with silver stripes (other ranks without stripes), the 2nd and 3rd Hussars wore grey overalls with a gold stripe for officers (no stripe for other ranks).

Line infantry officers wore grey trousers with silver stripes for officers, and infantry other ranks wore the same shoes and gaiters as the foot artillery.

Greatcoats for mounted troops were dark blue with large cape collars and for the dismounted arms, grey with no cape collar.

BADGES OF RANK

(a) *Generals.* Aiguillettes, gold chevrons on the lower arm and gold embroidery on cuffs, collars and chests.

(b) *Officers* (except hussars and light battalion officers who wore no distinguishing marks). Gold epaulettes with thick or thin fringes on both shoulders down through major. Captains – one gold epaulette on the right shoulder. Lieutenants – 'wings' of yellow or white scales on both shoulders.

(c) *Other ranks.* Chevrons on the right upper arm:

Sergeant-major – four and a crown
Sergeant – three
Corporal and cadet – two
Lance-corporal – one

Almost all officers wore waist-sashes which were gold and crimson silk for generals and crimson silk for all other officers. Sergeant-majors also had red worsted waist-sashes and also wore double-breasted jackets. Sergeants wore red worsted sashes having a central stripe in the facing colour.

The hussars and the 2nd Light Battalion wore hussar-type barrel sashes and the light dragoons a 'Pass gurtel' or 'stable-belt'.

For fatigues the men wore a blue cloth cap,

white waistcoat and drill trousers. Each commanding officer controlled his own regiment's fatigue dress.

Officers could also please themselves largely what they wore in camp: hats, trousers and boots were 'to taste'. For generals and staff officers there was a simple blue uniform without aiguillettes or embroidery.

Badges were also stamped on shoulder-belt plates.

Weapons

THE ARTILLERY

Foot batteries used 12- and 6-pounder guns and $5\frac{1}{2}$-inch howitzers.

Horse batteries used 3-pounder guns and $5\frac{1}{2}$-inch howitzers.

Barrel dimensions were:

	Weight	Length	Calibre	Normal charge of powder
6-pounder	$5\frac{1}{2}$ cwt	5 ft.	3·5 in.	$1\frac{1}{2}$ lb.
9-pounder	$13\frac{1}{2}$ cwt	6 ft.	4 in.	3 lb.
($15\frac{1}{2}$-pounder)				
$5\frac{1}{2}$-in. howitzer				
	13 cwt	4 ft. 8 in.	$5\frac{1}{2}$ in.	$2\frac{1}{2}$ lb.

The 9-pounder replaced the 12-pounder which was too heavy for good mobility in the field.

Shrapnel was first used in Spain in 1805.

Personal Weapons

HORSE ARTILLERY

Officers: curved sabres in steel scabbards on a black sling-belt, crimson and gold sword-knot, black sabretache, white leather bandolier (gold for parades) and pouch.

Other ranks: white sabre belt over the right shoulder, sabre with white leather fist strap, pistol in white holster with ammunition pouch attached.

FOOT ARTILLERY

Officers: sabres on white slings.

Other ranks: a white shoulder-belt on right shoulder carrying a short *Hirschfänger* (sword bayonet) in a leather scabbard. In addition six carbines were carried in clips on the limbers and each gunner had an ammunition pouch on his waist-belt.

CAVALRY

Officers of heavy dragoons had the heavy, straight sword with fist-guard of that arm in a steel scabbard on black slings. Other ranks had the same weapon on white slings, a carbine and a pistol.

When these two regiments were converted to light dragoons in 1813, they were rearmed as the hussars, i.e. curved sabre, with a single-bar fist-guard in a steel scabbard on black slings, two pistols and a carbine.

All cavalry carried black sabretaches and wore white bandoliers. Officers on parade wore silver or gold bandoliers and steel pouches. The officers of hussars had embroidered red cloth sabretaches. All officers and other ranks wore sword-knots as did the horse artillery.

The pistols were more for signalling than fighting; they had no sights and their maximum range was fifty paces. Carbines reached to 180 paces, were smooth-bored and inferior to the French model. Up to the time of the Peninsular War, the heavy dragoons carried a bayonet for their carbines.

Carbines hung from a clip on the bandolier with the muzzle, on the march, laid on the right holster cover and, when ready for action, in a boot behind the right heel of the rider.

Carbines had the same calibre as the pistol, thirty balls were carried in the pouch, the ball weighed $1\frac{1}{3}$ oz. and a normal powder charge was $\frac{3}{8}$ oz.

Infantry Weapons

Normal line infantry had the famous British 'Brown Bess' smooth-bore musket, sharpshooter and light battalions used the Baker rifled musket for one-third of their number, the other two-thirds using smooth-bores as for the line. Two calibres were thus used.

The rifle had seven grooves in the barrel with three-quarters of a turn. Its length with fixed *Hirschfänger* was 6 ft. $2\frac{1}{3}$ in. (4 ft. without bayonet)

It weighed 8 lb. 8½ oz. The backsight was set to 210–220 paces when at minimum, but could be set up to 300 paces with normal charge, or 400 paces if a patch was used.

A powder horn was carried by riflemen on a cord over the left shoulder and a powder measure in the breast pocket, together with a small water-bottle to dampen patches which were carried in a magazine in the butt of the weapon. A wooden mallet was carried in the haversack in order to assist in the loading of oversize balls.

The ramrod was attached to the rifleman by a cord so that it would not get lost in the heat of battle.

A rifleman had forty cartridges and twenty loose balls in his pouch; the musketeer sixty cartridges ready made up. The men used to cast their own balls. The 'Brown Bess' musket fired a 2 oz. ball with a powder charge of ⅝ oz. It was 4 ft. 9⅓ in. long (6 ft. 4¼ in. with fixed bayonet) and weighed 9 lb. 2 oz. (10 lb. 2 oz. with bayonet). There was a fixed back and foresight and maximum effective range was 120 paces. The bayonet was triangular and the whole weapon was considered better than the French 'M1777' musket.

Officers of light battalions carried the hussar sabre and wore a bandolier with signal whistle. N.C.O.s also had bandoliers and whistles.

Light battalion other ranks carried bayonets or *Hirschfänger* (according to the weapon they fired) in leather scabbards on their waist-belts.

Line infantry other ranks had bayonets in leather scabbards on a bandolier (except the sharpshooters who were equipped like the light battalion riflemen).

Line infantry officers carried their swords on white shoulder-belts called 'baldrics'. Pioneers, senior N.C.O.s, musicians and buglers carried carbines with a pouch for ten cartridges on their waist-belts.

Pioneers had short, wide, straight-bladed swords with saw-teeth along the back.

Cavalry Horse Furniture

HORSE ARTILLERY
An English saddle with blue, red-edged shabrack. Harness was brown. Drivers wore a padded wooden splint on the outside of their right legs to protect them against being crushed by the trail pole of the limber and carried leather whips.

HEAVY DRAGOONS
English saddles, blue shabrack with, for the 1st Regiment, black trim and the 2nd Regiment, red trim. (Officers wore gold-trimmed shabracks on parade.) Harness was brown with face cross-straps, crupper and breast-straps. On conversion to light dragoons, they adopted hussar harness.

All mounted men had portmanteaux (the artillery drivers carried theirs on the backs of the led horses).

HUSSARS
Bock saddles (light, wooden Hungarian or Turkish saddles) with, at first, a shabrack, later a sheepskin. Other details as for heavy dragoons.

Cleaning materials were carried (by those with English saddles) in a leather pouch opposite to the pistol holster, i.e. on the left. Hussars had two smaller pouches behind their holsters.

Rolled greatcoats were carried on the pommel.

A white linen haversack, blue wooden canteen forward on the saddle and a canvas feed-bag and cooking-pot behind completed the attachments, a picket rope being hung to the left rear of the saddle.

INFANTRY

Their packs were of canvas painted in the colour of their collars and contained underwear, washing and cleaning kit, a second pair of shoes, cloth cap and other spare clothing.

Greatcoats or blankets were rolled or folded and strapped on top of the pack. A metal cooking-cum-eating pot was also strapped on and a canvas haversack and blue wooden canteen completed their equipment.

Pioneers carried a shovel over one shoulder with its blade in a leather case and a saw or axe over the other. They wore a white or brown leather apron.

Hair and Beards

Pigtails remained until the Peninsular campaign (1809), but the heavy dragoons retained theirs until 1812. The men of the 3rd Hussars also wore black side-plaits up to and including the rank of corporal. Hussars of all ranks wore moustaches (and light dragoons from 1813 onwards). Other troops were only allowed side-whiskers. The exception to this rule was the 2nd Light Battalion (of Lieutenant-Colonel Colin Halkett) who wore moustaches throughout the battalion's existence.

Flags and Standards

Artillery, hussars and light battalions carried no colours. Each heavy dragoon regiment had one King's Standard and each of their squadrons had a guidon. Each King's Standard was crimson and square, and in the centre was a crown over the rose, thistle and shamrock surrounded by the Garter motto. In the two corners nearest the staff were the regimental initials and the white Hanoverian horse. Both sides of the standards were identical and they were edged in gold fringes.

The squadron guidons were fork tailed, gold fringed: dark blue for the 1st Regiment, black for the 2nd with similar embroidery to the King's Standard. The number of the squadron appeared below the central motif. All colours were carried by the youngest cornets and stood in the centre of the regiment or squadron.

Each line battalion had a King's colour and a battalion colour. The first was a Union Jack with 'King's German Legion' within a wreath all in gold in the centre, and the latter were dark blue having the Union Jack in the top staff corner and the battalion designation, in gold, in the centre of the flag.

Adolf Viktor Christian Jobst von Alten, born 2 November 1755, died 23 August 1820. In 1807 he accompanied his regiment of the Legion on the Baltic expedition, and in 1809, again as colonel commanding the 2nd Light Dragoons (Hussars), he went to the Scheldt estuary on the ill-fated Walcheren expedition. Subsequently he went to Spain, where his regiment fought under Wellington until 1814. Although present during the Waterloo campaign in Belgium, the 2nd Hussars were not engaged at Quatre Bras or Waterloo. Major-General von Alten, as he then was, commanded all the cavalry of the Legion during the campaign. In the portrait he seems to be wearing the uniform of the 2nd Hussars of the Legion, against a Spanish background

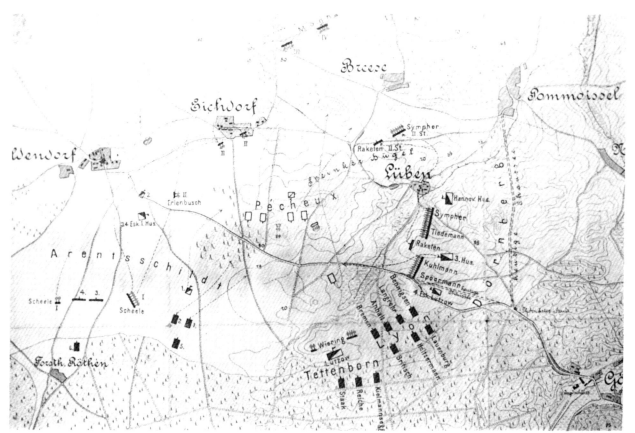

Battle Honours

These were worn on the shako plates and colours. All units but the 3rd and 8th Line battalions had 'Peninsular'. All units but the 6th and 7th Line battalions and the 2nd Hussars had 'Waterloo' (16–18 June 1815).

The 3rd Hussars and the two horse artillery batteries had 'Göhrde' (16 September 1813).

Both heavy dragoon regiments had 'Garcia Hernandez' (23 July 1812).

Both light battalions had 'Venta del Pozo' (23 October 1812).

The 1st Hussars had 'El Bodon' (25 September 1811).

The 2nd Hussars had 'Barrossa' (5 May 1811).

These battle honours were carried by the Prussian Army descendants of these units up until 1914.

Flagstaffs were brown, flagstaff tips brass and spear-shaped and being pierced to form a drooping, upright cross. Gold cords and tassels were fastened beneath the tip of the flagstaff and extended two-thirds of the way down the colour.

Plan of the Battle of the Göhrde. The Göhrde is a stream running into the Elbe, and the hamlet of the same name lies between Lüneburg and Dannenberg in the 'Dannenberger Zipfel', that peak of West German territory which today protrudes east into the German Democratic Republic. The French forces are indicated here by hollow squares, while the Anglo-Russo-German forces are the solid shapes. Both horse batteries and the 3rd Hussars of the Legion took part in this battle as complete units, as well as detachments from both light battalions, and the 1st, 2nd and 5th Line Battalions

SELECT BIBLIOGRAPHY

Ballauf, M., *The King's German Legion up to the Battle of Talavera, 28th of July 1809*.

Barrett, C. R. B., *The Cavalry of the King's German Legion*.

Beamish, Lieutenant-Colonel N. L., *History of the King's German Legion*.

Knötel, Herbert, and Sieg, Herbert, *Handbuch der Uniformkunde*, Hamburg, 1937.

Oman, C., *A History of the Peninsular War*.

Pfannkuche, A., *Die Geschichte der Königlich Deutsche Legion 1803–1816*.

Poten, Oberst B. von, *Die Geschichte der Königlich Deutsche Legion 1803–1816*.

Schaumann, A. L. F., *On the Road with Wellington*.

Schwertfeger, B., *Peninsula–Waterloo–In Erinnerung an der Königlich Deutsche Legion*.

The collections in the Lipperheide Sammlung, Berlin, the Bomann Museum, Celle, and the Historisches Museum in Hanover.

The Plates

A1 Corporal, 1st Heavy Dragoons, parade dress, 1808–13

The heavy dragoons of the Legion wore normal British heavy dragoon uniform, the coat shown here being based on an actual article shown in the Historisches Museum in the Pferdestrasse in Hanover. The yellow laces on the collar are each about three-quarters of an inch wide, the ten square-ended laces on the chest one inch wide, the yellow laces on cuffs and turnbacks half an inch wide. The corporal's rank stripes are gold on dark blue and were worn only on the right arm. A sergeant wore three such chevrons, a sergeant-major four chevrons and a crown. On each shoulder is a red 'wing' edged in half-inch yellow lace. The vertical pocket flap on the skirt is false and has three buttons. Unlike the infantry coat collars (which were worn open) the heavy dragoons wore their collars closed to the top. The white breeches are of leather; the heavy boots were not worn on campaigns but were replaced for field service by shorter boots worn under grey or dark blue overalls. The broad-bladed, heavy dragoon sword could inflict terrible wounds as the French found out to their cost.

In 1813 the two regiments of heavy dragoons were converted to light dragoons and received completely new uniforms and equipment.

A2 Officer, 2nd Heavy Dragoons, campaign dress, Spain 1812

Whereas the 1st Heavy Dragoons had dark blue facings, the 2nd had black; both regiments had yellow lace and buttons (gold for officers). On the shoulders the officer wears 'chain mail' of gilt rings on a black velvet backing with gold edging.

The white-over-red plume is worn in a black oilskin cover and the cumbersome bicorne is worn fore and aft (on parade it would be worn side to side) and the heavy brass chin scales would be tied under the chin in time of action.

The normal crimson silk waist-sash is worn, the badge of the British officer. The sword has a plain, white leather fist-strap, for parade wear this would have a gold and crimson tassel; for court wear the fist-strap was all gold and crimson.

A3 Trooper, 3rd Light Dragoons, parade dress, 1809

This figure is based on a sketch by Knötel. Until 1813 the three regiments of light dragoons of the Legion wore the uniform shown here, the facings being 1st Regiment – red, 2nd Regiment – white, and 3rd Regiment – yellow. There was a white edging to collar, lapels and cuffs and all buttons were white. The helmet was low in the crown and had a crest of black bearskin for officers, black horsehair for other ranks. On the right-hand side

An illuminated scroll issued in 1862 to mark the fiftieth anniversary of the clash at Garcia-Hernandez on 22–23 July 1812, in the aftermath of Wellington's victory at Salamanca. The 1st and 2nd Heavy Dragoons of the Legion won immortal glory by breaking two fully formed enemy infantry squares, an occurrence of extreme rarity in the Napoleonic Wars. The script reads: 'Lord Wellington said in his official report: "I have never seen a bolder cavalry charge than that executed by the heavy cavalry brigade of the King's German Legion under major-general von Bock against the enemy infantry. The success of this charge was complete, the entire infantry of the 1st Division, consisting of three battalions, were captured."' The scroll was issued by the officers of the Hanoverian Garde du Corps, the descendants of the 1st Heavy Dragoons of the Legion

of the helmet was a brass badge of a crown over a circular plate bearing the inscription KING'S GERMAN LEGION and the regimental number; on the left-hand side was a white-over-red plume. The turban was dark blue and held by brass chains. Across the peak was a brass strip bearing the regimental designation. The epaulettes were white worsted for other ranks, silver for officers. The bandoliers supported the ammunition pouch and the carbine, the waist-belt carried the light cavalry curved sabre in a steel sheath on slings.

In 1813 the light dragoons of the Legion were converted to hussars and were completely re-uniformed as such, retaining only their facing colours in their new role.

B1 Trooper, 2nd Light Dragoons, field service dress, 1814–16

Upon their conversion from heavy dragoons to light dragoons, both regiments received dark blue coats with red facings shown on collar, lapels, pointed cuffs, turnbacks and pocket flap edgings. A dark blue waist-sash with two red stripes was worn and the grey overalls had twin red stripes down the legs. The 1st Regiment had yellow buttons and epaulettes (gold for officers), the 2nd white (silver for officers). Other ranks wore their ranks in the form of chevrons, point down, in the facing colour on the upper right arm; corporals had two chevrons, sergeants three and sergeant-majors four chevrons and a crown.

Instead of the straight, heavy cavalry sword, the men now carried the curved, light cavalry sabre. The device on the front of the shako was rather like a spoked wheel. The white leather bandoliers supported pouch and carbine; the sabre was suspended from slings on a waist-belt. It is interesting to see that the light dragoons wore sabretaches at this time. The cap lines were long and ended in 'flounders' and tassels which were passed under the right epaulette. Chin-scales were brass.

B2 Officer, 1st Hussars, parade dress, 1813–16

Although the light dragoon regiments of the British Army had been subtitled 'Hussars' for some years, their change of costume to comply with this title lagged behind.

In 1813 the three light dragoon regiments of the Legion were retitled and reuniformed as hussars, although they now presented a somewhat confusing sartorial picture. The 1st Hussars wore brown busbies (fur 'Kolpaks' with a red bag and no peak); the 2nd Hussars wore what can only be described as 'brown fur shakos', conical in shape and having a black leather peak as well as a red bag; and in the 3rd Hussars the officers wore brown fur shakos with red bag and black peak while the troopers wore shakos in black felt, as did the two light dragoon regiments.

For all three regiments dolmans and pelisses were dark blue and the waist-sash was crimson with yellow barrels (gold for officers). All sabre-taches were plain black leather for other ranks, those of the officers having gold lace embroidery and the crowned gold cipher G R.

B3 Officer, 2nd Hussars, parade dress, 1813–16

As an identifying peculiarity, the 2nd Regiment wore two yellow laces and buttons (gold for officers) on each side of its white dolman collar. Officers' bandoliers were gold edged in red, other ranks wore white leather bandoliers. For parade wear the three hussar regiments had dark blue shabracks edged in the facing colour, otherwise they wore black sheepskin saddle rugs edged in the facing colour, this edging having a 'wolfstooth' or 'Vandyke' shape along the outer edge.

C1 Officer, Foot Artillery, parade dress, 1812–16

Originally, the foot artillery officers of the Legion had a slightly different uniform without the gold laces on the red lapels or the loop on the collar. This was replaced in about 1807 by the uniform shown above. The single gold epaulette indicates a lieutenant, a captain wore two such epaulettes with light fringes, field officers (majors and above) two epaulettes with heavy fringes. The officers of foot artillery were mounted and wore spurs and carried curved, light cavalry sabres on black slings.

C2 Officer, 1st Light Battalion, field service uniform, 1808–16

Unlike their men, the officers of the 1st Light Battalion wore no cap-badges on their conical shakos, the only decorations being the black silk cords, the black silk cockade held by a silver button, and the black pompon and tuft which surmounted the cockade.

The dark green coatee hooked together down the front, the two rows of buttons being only for decoration. On the black collar and cuffs was simple black lace decoration, the parade coatee having much more elaborate black lace decoration extending up both sleeves. On the shoulders are silver 'chain mail' wings on black velvet backing, the plain black lacquered leather bandolier and pouch would be replaced by items decorated with silver for parade wear. The officer is shown with the parade sabre-strap, i.e. white leather strap, gold and crimson tassel. The trousers have a silver side stripe.

C3 Drummer, Foot Artillery, 1812–16
The artillery of the Legion were dressed exactly as for their British counterparts (apart from titles on cap-plates, buttons, packs, etc.). As part of those forces controlled by the Board of Ordnance as opposed to those controlled by the 'Horse Guards' (cavalry and infantry), the artillery wore blue uniforms with red facings and yellow buttons and lace. For the foot artillery this lace was 'bastion ended' – musicians and drummers wearing yellow epaulettes, gunners having red shoulder-straps edged yellow. Being artillery the gunners carried short, wide-bladed swords which were useful in clearing a way for the guns through close country. Badges of rank were the usual chevrons, in gold, on the upper right arm.

D1 Rifleman, 2nd Light Battalion, field service marching order, 1815
This is the costume worn on the battlefield of Waterloo. The light battalions of the Legion were equipped with the British Baker rifle and the sword-bayonet (which German riflemen call a *Hirschfänger*). Even today, the British rifle battalions use the expression 'sword' when referring to the bayonet of the self-loading rifle on drill parades.

Whereas the men of the 1st Light Battalion had a small, black, round pompon and a black tuft on their shakos, those of the 2nd Light Battalion had only a larger, black, round pompon. The 2nd Light Battalion wore dark green dolmans (hussar jackets without skirts) having three rows of white spherical buttons and black shoulder-straps and tufts (as for the centre companies of a line batta-

lion in shape) while the 1st Light Battalion had single-breasted dark green coats with very short skirts, other ranks a single row of white spherical buttons, and black shoulder-rolls or wings.

The black-painted canvas pack bore a white bugle badge over the battalion number and the standard British issue, light blue, flat, round wooden canteen also showed the owner's unit – K.G.L. 2 L.B. – in black paint.

Officers of the 2nd Light Battalion had rows of black silk lace across the chests of their dark green dolmans and instead of the conical shako they wore a 'mirliton' or winged cap with a small square peak which could be folded up or down. The mirliton was part of the historical costume of the Hungarian (Austrian) hussars. Apart from these items, the officers of both battalions dressed alike. The 2nd Light Battalion was the only infantry unit in the British Army allowed to wear moustaches.

D2 Private, centre companies, line infantry battalions, parade dress, 1803–08
The man is shown wearing the 'stovepipe' shako which was worn in the British Army from 1801 until it was superseded in 1812 by the 'Waterloo' shako. Although Beamish and Schwertfeger show all-white plumes for centre companies, the plates in their books are very small and contain other inaccuracies. It is thus almost certain that the plumes of the line battalions were exactly as in the British Army, i.e. grenadier company – all white; centre companies – white over red; light company – dark green. The hair was rolled, queued and powdered until 1808 when the British Army abolished the queue and had hair cut short.

As a centre company man, his shoulder-straps end in white worsted tufts, the flank companies (grenadiers and light) having red 'wings' (edged and striped in white lace and edged with white worsted tufts) in addition to the centre companies' white tufts. Although some sources state that the white lace of the King's German Legion had a 'blue worm' in it, none of the uniforms in Celle show any such decoration and the 'Aertz' pictures confirm that the lace was plain except for drummers and musicians. The brass cap-plate bears the crown over the cipher 'GR', under this an ova 'belt' inscribed KING'S GERMAN LEGION with the battalion number in the centre of the oval. The belt-plate bears an oval 'belt' inscribed KING'S GERMAN LEGION, above the belt a lion, within the belt a crown. The buttons are of pewter, half rounded, about three-quarters of an inch in diameter and are stamped with a crown above K.G.L., and below this the battalion number.

D3 Private, centre companies, line battalions, field service marching order, 1812–16

Although details of the back of the jacket are obscured by the equipment, these may be seen in the black and white illustrations of this book. The 'Waterloo shako', which was issued from 1812 onwards, is clearly shown and is reputed to have been modelled on the headgear of the Portuguese line infantry of that time. The cockade and plume have now been moved to the left-hand side of the shako, cords are worn across the front and end in tassels on the right-hand side, and the front flap extends above the top of the headpiece; the brass badge-plate is unchanged.

In the later stages of the Peninsular campaign, British troops were issued with blankets instead of greatcoats, and these blankets were so designed as to permit them to be fastened together to form a tent.

E1 Bugler of sharpshooters of a line battalion, field service marching order, 1812–16

Here all the appointments of the sharpshooters of the line battalions can clearly be seen: the green plume and cords to the shako and the red wings on the shoulders. Also clearly visible is the blue and white lace worn by drummers, buglers and musicians. I suspect that the bugler's rifle would not be carried in action but would be left behind with the company baggage as a reserve weapon to replace battle losses. A bugler's task was to attend his officer and to give commands by use of his bugle: this he cannot do if he is involved in the tactical battle.

E2 Sergeant-major, line battalion, parade dress, 1812–16

Being the senior non-commissioned rank in the battalion, the sergeant-major's uniform was a mixture of officer's dress (the double-breasted coat, the crimson silk sash, the sword and fist-strap, the gold collar lace and the gold shako cords and trouser seam) and that of the men (the short skirts to the coat, the shoulder-straps). The rank badges were in gold, edged in the facing colour.

E3 Colour-bearer 5th Line Battalion, parade dress, 1815–16

This officer, an ensign, is carrying the battalion flag of the 5th Battalion. Prior to the First World War, many of the flags of the King's German Legion (then the personal property of the Duke of Cambridge) were given over to the Vaterlandisches Museum in Hanover. These flags are presently stored in the Historisches Museum, am Hohen Ufer, Pferdestrasse 6, in Hanover, together with numerous other relics of the Legion.

F Officer, Horse Artillery, parade dress, 1808–16

Apart from the demise of the pigtail in 1808, this uniform remained practically unchanged during the Legion's existence. As with the British horse artillery (whose uniforms were almost exactly the same as those shown and described here), the Legion Horse Artillery wore the British 'light dragoon' helmet and hussar-pattern dolman and pelisse. Officers had sabretaches, but the mounted gunners did not. As was popular in England at this time, the horses' tails were docked.

G1 Trooper, 3rd Hussars, parade dress, 1813–16

The illustrated uniform is based on a watercolour in the Bomann Museum in Celle and on an actual dolman of the regiment which is also in that museum. The initially strange combination of hussar uniform and shako may well have been the result of shortages in the supply of the right kind of fur.

G2 Janissary, 1st Light Battalion, parade dress

As was popular with many armies of the day, the British frequently employed Negroes ('Moors') as musicians in their regimental bands. His parade costume is a mixture of North African and Hungarian – altogether most exotic!

G3 Mounted Gunner, Horse Artillery, field dress, 1808–16

The uniform jacket shown here is almost exactly the same as that worn today by the King's Troop, Royal Horse Artillery, on ceremonial occasions.

The horse furniture of the Peninsular days consisted of a dark blue shabrack with pointed rear corners, edged with a broad red stripe and a rectangular-ended, dark blue portmanteau, the ends of which are outlined in red and bear the cipher in red: $\overset{KGA}{2}$ (the numeral is the battery number).

For parades, close-fitting white breeches and short hussar-type boots with screw-in steel spurs were worn.

H1 Officer of sharpshooters, line battalions, parade dress, 1812–16

Instead of the epaulettes worn by officers of the centre companies of the line battalions, officers of the flank companies wore 'wings' of gilt chain on dark blue velvet backing edged with gold. The dark green shako plume and the curved sabre on black slings indicate an officer of sharpshooters. The white pouch belt is also a connection back to the dress of officers of the light battalions and thus (further extended) back to the hussars or light cavalry whose function the light infantry took over in the dismounted role.

H2 Corporal of sharpshooters of the line battalions, skirmishing order, 1812–16

For non-commissioned officers up to the rank of colour-sergeant, chevrons were of white lace on the upper right arm. For skirmishing duties the corporal has left his pack and blanket with the company baggage; he retains his water canteen, ammunition pouch and powder horn which is carried on the dark green cord attached to his ammunition pouch bandolier. The small pouch on his belt is his patch pouch.

H3 Sergeant of a light battalion, 'undress' walking-out dress, 1808–16

This is undoubtedly the old waistcoat of former days, now elevated to the status of a garment fit to be seen in public. The black hat with edging and band in dark green was probably made up from old jackets. It is quite likely that the line battalions had similar headgear in dark blue and red which they had made up by their tailors. The cane was once the sign of office of an N.C.O.; officers of the British Army still carry such items today, each regiment having its own peculiar pattern.

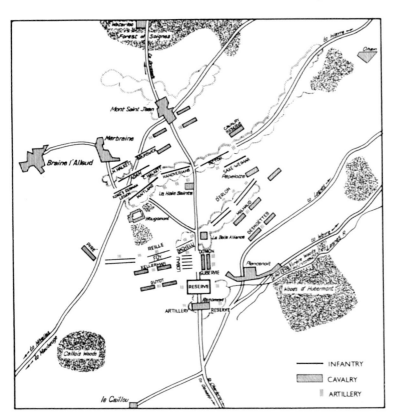

The Battle of Waterloo, 18 June 1815

INDEX

Figures in **bold** refer to illustrations.